Epochs of Indian History

ANCIENT INDIA

Epochs of Indian History

ANCIENT INDIA

2000 B.C.- 800 A. D.

ROMESH CHUNDER DUTT, C.I.E., I.C.S.

WITH TWO MAPS

GYAN

Published by

GYAN

Gyan Publishing House
5, Ansari Road
Darayaganj, New Delhi-110002
Phone: 011-47034999, 9811692060
E-mail: books@gyanbooks.com

Distribution Network
gyanbooks.com
India, USA, Canada, UK, Australia, France

ISBN: 978-81-212-9322-8 (PB)
First Published, 1893

2nd Impression 2023

Printed at: Gyan Press, Delhi.

EPOCHS OF INDIAN HISTORY ANCIENT INDIA

Author: ROMESH CHUNDER DUTT

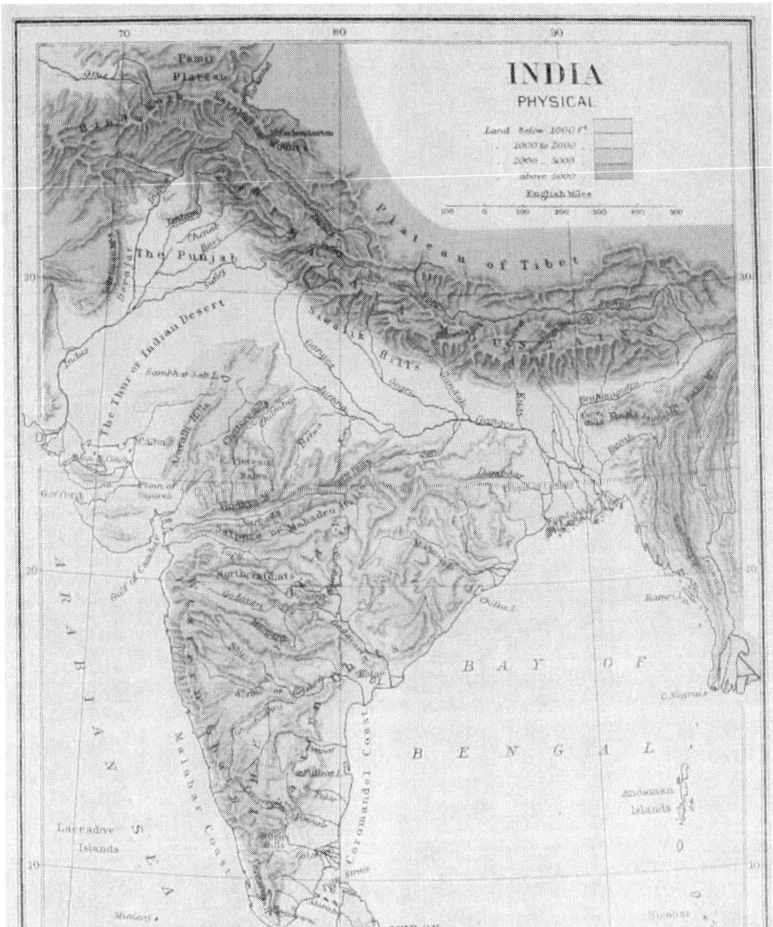

Longmans Green & Co. London, New York & Bombay

EPOCHS OF INDIAN HISTORY

EDITED BY

JOHN ADAM, M.A.

PRINCIPAL OF PACHAIYAPPA'S COLLEGE, AND FELLOW OF THE UNIVERSITY, MADRAS; SOMETIME SCHOLAR OF PEMBROKE COLLEGE, CAMBRIDGE

ANCIENT INDIA

2000 B.C.–800 A.D.

Epochs of Indian History

ANCIENT INDIA

2000 B.C.–800 A.D.

BY

ROMESH CHUNDER DUTT, C.I.E., I.C.S.

BARRISTER-AT-LAW, FELLOW OF THE UNIVERSITY OF CALCUTTA
MEMBER OF THE ASIATIC SOCIETY OF BENGAL
AUTHOR OF "A HISTORY OF CIVILIZATION IN ANCIENT INDIA", ETC.

WITH TWO MAPS

NEW IMPRESSION

LONGMANS, GREEN, AND CO.
39 PATERNOSTER ROW, LONDON
NEW YORK AND BOMBAY
1904

EDITOR'S PREFACE.

THE present volume is the first of a series of EPOCHS OF INDIAN HISTORY. To write a history of India on the scale of a Freeman, or even of a Macaulay, would, from the multiplicity and diversity of detail, be a task of superhuman magnitude. The story of India during the past four thousand years is the story not of one country but of many countries, not of one nation but of many nations, told not in one language but in many languages, and influenced in turn by the greatest religions of the world. In consequence we find the best historical work in the Indian field is bestowed upon special periods or particular areas. The result is evident in the shorter histories which attempt to cover the whole ground. There is a universal want of balance; the writer insensibly, but inevitably, brings to the front the epoch he has studied in detail, or the district where his experience has been gained. The present Series will endeavour to correct this tendency by assigning each epoch to a writer who has made it a subject of special research; while it will be the task of the Editor to endeavour to preserve continuity on the one hand and to prevent overlapping on the other.

The volume now published summarizes the history of ancient India,—or more properly, of those northern regions that first came under the influence of Aryan civilization—down to the time when the Hindu sovereignties were swept away for ever by Muhammadan invaders from the north. The history of those invaders and of the dynasties they founded will form the subject of another volume. Southern India—the Dravidian Peninsula—long maintained an independent civilization. It never was—it is not yet—more than partially Aryanized; the Moslem occasionally raided through but never remained. On its shores, too, the European explorer first set his foot, and within its territories French and English had their final struggle for Eastern Empire. The history of Drávida, down to the time when the death of Tippu Sultán made it irretrievably a British Province, will thus naturally constitute a thira epoch. Between North and South lies the middle land of the Dekhan. It, too, nas a history of its own. At first the wilderness of Dandaka, peopled with strange monsters; later the home of the conquering Andhras; subsequently the debatable land whence it was the ambition of every warlike follower of the Prophet to carve for himself a kingdom; and finally the seat of the Hindu empire of the Mahrattas,—its story furnishes a fourth epoch. The end of the Mysore wars, the overthrow of the Mahratta power, and the pensioning of the Moghul kings of Delhi, occurring as they do within a period of twenty years, mark the definite establishment of the British Ráj throughout all India south of the Himálayas; and therefore the history of British India will be the history of India in the nineteenth century.

While it is hoped that the political history of the various epochs will be found sufficient for the student and in accordance with the latest results of research, the first aim of the writers will be to give a history of the Indian people, to follow the varied development of institutions and constitutions, to mark the growth and decay of literature and science, to watch the constant flux of law and religion. It is not perhaps too much to hope that a truer knowledge of the not inglorious past of the races who, in the inscrutable course of events, have come under the dominion of the people of Great Britain, will help to make the bonds between the two nations closer and more enduring than any that the power of the sword alone can forge. Though in the execution the measure of success may vary, the same spirit and purpose will animate the different volumes of the Series.

J. A.

TABLE OF CONTENTS.

NOTE.

The spelling of proper names is according to the system authorized by the Government of India, except in the case of a few well-known words, as Punjab, where a change from the authorized form would be pedantic. The accent marks a long vowel, and all the vowels are sounded as in the Latin languages.

ANCIENT INDIA.

EPOCH I.—VEDIC AGE.

HINDU SETTLEMENTS ON THE INDUS.
B.C. 2000–1400.

CHAPTER I.

INTRODUCTION.

IT has been observed, with much truth, that the early civilization of mankind was determined by natural causes, or, in other words, by the fertilizing power of great rivers and by the influence of a warm and genial climate, conducive alike to the production of crops and to the comfort of man. Other causes have exerted a greater influence in more modern times, and a temperate or cold climate has fostered the more robust civilization of these days; but in the remote past we shall seek in vain for the first glimpses of human civilization except on favoured spots, where Nature helped man by copious and fertilizing inundations, and a warm and genial climate.

Modern researches have shown that between thirty and forty centuries ago, civilization was not the common property of the human race, but was confined almost exclusively to four favoured spots in the Old World. The valley of the Nile was the seat of a powerful empire, and of a very ancient civilization The valley of the Euphrates and the Tigris similarly witnessed the civilization of powerful Semitic nations—the Assyrians, and the Babylonians—flourishing within its confines and imparting its light to surrounding regions The valley of the Hoang Ho and the Yangse Kiang was similarly the home of an ancient Turanian civilization which flourishes to this day after the lapse of thousands of years. And lastly, the valley of the Indus and its tributaries witnessed the earliest form of civilization developed by a section of those Aryan races,* who in the present day rule the world, and carry civilization to the remotest portions of the globe So universal is the fact of civilization, in these days, that it is difficult to conceive that it was confined to four isolated spots in the world only a hundred generations ago , and that the vast spaces between these favoured and very limited areas were filled by swarms of hunting and pastoral tribes, warring against each other, migrating in hordes with their tents and cattle from place to place, leaving no trace of their movements or their national existence in the records of history, leaving no mark in the annals of human progress, literature, and science

* Recent anthropological discoveries have proved that the nations which are known as the Aryan races in Europe and in Asia, viz., the Teutons the Celts the Slavs, the Italics, the Hellenes the Persians, the Hindus, &c , are not all actually descended from the same stock, although they speak languages derived from the same ancient tongue, of which the Sanscrit language is the oldest and nearest specimen It is supposed that the primitive Aryans dwellers probably of Central Asia and Eastern Europe, spread their conquests on all sides and imposed their language on nations whose descendants still speak modifications of the same tongue It is convenient to speak of these Aryan speaking nations of the modern day as Aryan nations. The Hindus claim that they are actually descended from the primitive Aryan stock.

The history of civilization, of the infant civilization of mankind, belongs to these four countries. The light has broadened and expanded as the day has advanced, but mankind will ever look back with interest on the misty dawn of civilization, on the small beginnings of progress and knowledge, for which the enlightened and mighty nations of the modern world are indebted to the early shepherds and cultivators of Egypt and Babylonia, of China and India. To Greece and to Rome belongs the credit of catching the light from the East, and reflecting it with tenfold lustre on the West.

In studying the history of the earliest civilized nations of the world, we are unable to fix dates, or to trace the course of events with the degree of accuracy which marks modern history, or even the history of Rome and Greece. But nevertheless we possess sufficient materials with regard to the earlier nations to ascertain the general course of events, to mark the great results achieved from age to age, and to trace the progress of knowledge, literature, and science, through the successive epochs of their national existence.

If this is true of Egypt, and Babylonia, and China, it is still more so in respect of India. The hieroglyphic records of the Egyptians tell us about ancient kings and pyramid-builders, of dynasties, invasions, and wars. The cuneiform inscriptions of Assyria and Babylon tell us much the same kind of story. And even the ancient records of China tell us more about kings and dynasties than about the progress and civilization of the people.

The ancient Hindu works, with which Europe has become familiar within the last hundred years, are of a different character. They tell us little of kings and dynasties; and even when such lists are available, they are bare lists of names, and have little value in a true historical sense. On the other hand, the copious literature which we possess, and which belongs to the different epochs of Hindu history, presents a faithful picture of Hindu life and civilization through the successive periods of their natural existence. And thus the ancient works form a connected and comprehensive history of the Hindu nation for four thousand years, so full, so clear, that he who runs may read.

Inscriptions on stone and writings on papyri are recorded with a design to commemorate passing events. The songs and poetry and religious compositions of a people are an unconscious and true reflection of their civilization and thought. The earliest effusions of the Hindus were not recorded in writing; they are therefore full and unrestricted—they are a natural and true expression of the nation's thoughts and feelings. They were preserved, not on stone or papyri, but in the faithful memory of the people, who handed down the sacred heritage from century to century with a scrupulous exactitude which in modern days would be considered a miracle. For several centuries this ancient literature was thus preserved in the nation's memory, until writing was introduced, and the literature was recorded; but even then teachers preferred to teach, and students to learn, by rote, and it was considered a sin to learn sacred texts from written works. Later literature sprang up in following ages, and lies, strata upon strata, over the more ancient literature of India, as clearly distinguishable from each other to the historian, as the different strata of rocks are to the geologist. European antiquarians have during the last hundred years examined this great mass of literature, have sifted and classified it, and have assigned to each class of works its proper age; and thus classified and examined, the literature tells a continuous and most interesting story of a nation's life and progress through forty centuries. It is the story of an Aryan people, at first isolated by situation and circumstances from the outside world, and working out its own religious and social institutions, its literature, laws, and science; and it forms one of the most instructive and interesting chapters in the annals of human progress and culture.

This wonderful story divides itself into several well-defined Epochs or Periods, and five of these epochs belong to ancient history. It is desirable in this introductory chapter to make a brief mention of these five epochs.

I. Vedic Epoch.

Hindu Settlements on the Indus, B.C. 2000–1400.

The history of the Hindus begins with their settlement in the Punjab and their conquest of that province from the dark-skinned aborigines. This war of conquest and colonization went on for centuries; and the obstinate and brave children of the soil were beaten back from river to river and from fastness to fastness. The interminable forests were gradually cleared, fair villages and hamlets surrounded by smiling fields of corn arose on the banks of the fertilizing streams, Hindu forms of worshipping the "bright gods" of Nature by oblations to the fire were established, and Hindu civilization at last spread itself throughout the land of the "seven rivers", from the Indus to the Sarasvatí. A great division had in the meantime broken out in the Aryan camp. A section of that race protested against animal sacrifices and the use of the fermented Soma wine, and these puritans retired from the Punjab westwards to the Irán, where they formed the ancient Persian race, and founded the Parsi religion.

It is not possible with any degree of accuracy to fix the dates of these events. "Four thousand years ago," says

Professor Max Müller, "or it may be earlier, the Aryans who had travelled southwards to the rivers of the Punjab, called him (their Supreme Deity) Dyaush-Pitá or Heavenly Father," answering to the Jupiter of the Romans. The hymns which were composed by the early Aryan conquerors of the Punjab to Dyaush-Pitá and the other bright gods of Nature are still preserved to us in the compilation known as the *Rig Veda;* and we may safely fix the period between 2000 and 1400 B.C. as the approximate age of these ancient hymns. We may roughly accept these six centuries as the first epoch of Hindu history, the epoch of Hindu settlements on the Indus and its tributaries.

II. Epic Epoch.

Hindu Kingdoms on the Ganges, B.C. 1400–1000.

From the Punjab the Hindus began to pour down along the course of the Ganges, until in a few centuries the whole of the Gangetic basin, from the Northern mountains to Benáres and Behar, became the seat of brave, martial, and civilized nations. Indeed, these vigorous colonists soon left their mother-land, the Punjab, in the shade; and the picture we possess of the cultured Gangetic races, with their brilliant courts and schools of learning, with their great tournaments and feats of arms, and with their elaborate social rules and religious rites, testifies to a state of civilization far in advance of that of their sturdy forefathers of the Punjab. Prominent among the Gangetic races were the Kurus, who settled on the upper course of the Ganges, to the east of the site of modern Delhi, and their great rivals the Panchálas, who settled lower down the stream, not far from the site of modern Kanouj. Lower down the same river lived the Kásís, near modern Benáres; still further down the stream, and to the north of it, the Videhas dwelt in modern Tirhút; while between the Kurus and the Videhas lived the powerful Kosalas in modern Oudh. These and other races had their mutual jealousies, their varying alliances, and their internecine wars, but were nevertheless bound together by a common sacred language and literature, by a common religion, and by common social and religious institutions. The student of Greek history is tempted to compare these flourishing and civilized Gangetic states with the Greek cities in their palmy days, while he would compare the sturdy but less civilized Hindu settlers on the banks of the Indus with the robust Greek warriors who fought with the Trojans. The ascendency and vigour of the Gangetic kingdoms lasted for four or five centuries.

III. RATIONALISTIC EPOCH.

Hindu Expansion over all India, B.C. *1000–320.*

When Northern India as far as Benáres and North Behar had been occupied, colonies began to be established in more distant places, and the whole of India became thus Hinduized in the course of some centuries. South Behar or Magadha was early civilized; schools of philosophy multiplied in this age, and in the sixth century before Christ, Gautama Buddha preached there the great religion which is now the religion of a third of the human race. Malwa or Avanti became a seat of culture or learning; while beyond the Vindhya mountains the Andhras had a great and powerful kingdom in the Dekhan, stretching as far down as the Kistna river, and boasting of a great capital and of celebrated schools of learning. Colonists from the banks of the Jumna and the Ganges settled in Gujrat and founded the ancient seaport of Dvaraka; and it is supposed that merchants from this place sailing to the extreme south of India helped to civilize the kingdom of Pandya. Certain it is that by the fourth century before Christ, three sister nations, the Pandyas, the Cholas, and the Cheras, had established powerful kingdoms in India, south of the Kistna river. In the east, Anga or East Behar, Vanga or Bengal, and Kalinga or Orissa, also received the light of Hindu civilization, religion, and literature, while the distant island of Ceylon was conquered and Hinduized in the fifth century.

Thus all India, except wilds and deserts, had received Hindu civilization, manners, and religion, before the time of Alexander the Great. It is necessary, however, to make a passing remark about these southern Hindu kingdoms, as distinguished from the older northern kingdoms. The Aryan races had penetrated in vast numbers into the Punjab and the Gangetic valley, and had all but exterminated or expelled the children of the soil, who were utter barbarians ; and the population of Northern India therefore is, to the present day, more or less of pure Aryan stock. On the other hand, the later and less numerous Hindu colonists who penetrated into South Behar and Bengal, to the Dekhan and Southern India, found the aboriginal races of those spacious regions possessing a more or less imperfect civilization of their own, and the extermination of those vast populations all over India by a handful of colonists was out of the question. The Hindu colonists were satisfied therefore with introducing Hindu civilization, language, and religion ; and to this day the majority of the population of Southern and Eastern India are of non-Aryan stock who have adopted the higher civilization, literature, and religion of their Aryan Hindu conquerors and teachers.

The Hindu world of the third Epoch, *i.e.*, of the sixth, fifth, and fourth centuries B.C., thus appears to us as a map coloured in two or three different shades, representing different degrees of Aryan enlightenment. Northern India is almost purely Aryan, while the Southern and Eastern Indian states are more or less non-Aryan, with a veneer of Aryan religion and civilization cast over them. It is remarkable that the ancient Hindu writers of the sixth and fifth centuries before Christ viewed India in this light, and one of them parcels out the Hindu world into three portions to indicate the degrees of their Aryan purity. Northern India comes first; South and East Behar, Malwa, Gujrat, and the Dekhan are included by him in the second portion; while Bengal, Orissa, and India south of the Kistna are included in the last. If we were disposed to find a parallel to the Hindu world of the third Epoch, we should compare it with the Greek world after the death of Alexander, when outside Greece proper, Macedon, Egypt, and the whole of Western Asia wore the livery of Greek civilization, religion, and literature.

IV. Buddhist Epoch.

Ascendency of Magadha, B.C. 320–A.D. 400.

If the first three Epochs of Hindu history are epochs of the gradual expansion of the Hindus first over the Punjab, then in the Gangetic valley, and then over all India, the fourth is the Epoch of a union among these Hindu races under a great and dominant ruling power. Immediately after the departure of Alexander the Great from India, the great Chandragupta founded a new dynasty in Magadha, and for the first time united the whole of Northern India under his vigorous rule. His grandson, Asoka the Great, adopted Buddhism as the state religion in the third century before Christ, even as Constantine the Great adopted the Christian religion in the fourth century after Christ. The dynasty of Chandragupta and Asoka declined in course of time; but the powerful Andhras of the Dekhan took possession of Magadha about the commencement of the Christian era, and down to the close of the fourth century after Christ held the supreme power both in Northern and Southern India. After the fourth century the Andhras declined, and the ascendency of the Magadha Empire was at an end.

We may consider the first three Epochs of the History of Ancient India as a preparation for the fourth Epoch. In the former, all India was gradually civilized and Hinduized; in the last, it was united under one great central power, even as Europe and Western Asia were united in the same age under the imperial power of Rome.

V. PURANIC EPOCH.

Ascendency of Kanouj and Ujain, A.D. 400–800.

The parallel between Hindu history and European history extends further than would appear at first sight. The supreme power passed from the rulers of Magadha to the emperors of Kanouj and Ujain in the fifth and succeeding centuries, but like the later Roman emperors they had to battle against hordes of barbarian invaders to save their country and their civilization. The war went on for centuries, and races of barbarians settled down in the west and south of India, and adopted Hindu manners, religion, and civilization. But the crisis came, and ancient Hindu rule was at last swept away from Northern India in the eighth century. Ancient Hindu history terminates at this date.

Dark ages followed in India as in Europe, and the history of Northern India in the ninth and tenth centuries is a perfect blank. Towards the close of the tenth century, a new power arose on the ruins of ancient civilization in Europe and in India; the feudal barons in Europe, and the Rajpút barons in India. These new Rajpút chiefs stepped into the vacant thrones of ancient and polished but effete nations, and adopted the Hindu religion and civilization, even as the mediæval kings and conquerors of Europe embraced the Christian faith. And the new defenders of Hinduism and of Christianity had to fight in India and in Europe against the same rising power, viz., the Muhammadans. But here the parallel ends. After centuries of warfare, the Christian knights beat back the Moslems from France, from Spain, and from Austria. The Rajpút chiefs of India offered an equally brave, but not an equally successful, resistance; they struggled and they fell; and Hindu independence and national life terminated with the conquest of India by the Muhammadans.

Historical analogies are often misleading unless we constantly bear in mind the great differences in details, even when the resemblance in the outline seems most striking. But when instituted with due caution, such comparisons have their use; and they show us how the same historical laws rule the destinies and the progress of nations at the farthest ends of the globe, and how the same great historical causes often affect and control the march of events, simultaneously in the east and the west.

CHAPTER II.

WARS WITH THE ABORIGINES.

THE history of the first Epoch, which we have called the Vedic Age, is the history of the conquest of the Punjab from the aborigines. And although we have no connected account left to us of the main incidents of this war of centuries, yet the Rig Veda—the collection of hymns composed in this early age—is full of stirring passages and martial songs, which enable us to realize the warlike ardour of the Hindu colonists and conquerors of the Punjab. They cleared the primeval forests, beat back or exterminated the dark-skinned children of the soil, widened the limits of cultivation and of civilization, and spread Hindu dominion and Hindu religion from generation to generation, and from century to century. The story of the extermination of barbarians by civilized races is much the same in ancient and in modern times; and the banks of the Indus and its tributaries were cleared of their aborigines eighteen hundred years before Christ, much in the same way in which the banks of the great Mississippi have been cleared, eighteen hundred years after Christ, of the many brave and warlike Indian tribes, who lived, and ruled, and hunted in the primeval woods of America. The white man came with a higher civilization, with a purer religion but also with a greed of conquest; he cleared trackless and impenetrable forests, built fair villages and towns on the sites of fastnesses and swamps, and turned a dark and unexplored continent into haunts of civilized men, and the seat of purer forms of religion, society, and government. The dark man had no place in this new world; he perished, struggling bravely but vainly in his last fastness, or he left the land and fled to wilder and remoter regions, as yet untrod by the white conquerors.

Indra, the rain-giving sky, is also the martial deity of the conquering Hindus, and in the hymns addressed to this deity we find numerous invocations for help against the dark aborigines called the *Dasyu* or the *Dasa*, who fought with all the obstinacy and skill of barbarians. A few such passages will give us a true and realistic idea of this obstinately contested war of centuries.

"Indra, invoked by many, and accompanied by his fleet companions, has destroyed by his thunderbolt the *Dasyus* and *Simyus* who dwelt on earth, and distributed the fields to his white worshippers. The thunderer makes the sun shine, and the rain descend."—*Rig Veda*, I 100, 18.

"Indra with his thunderbolt, and full of vigour, has destroyed the towns of the *Dasyus* and wandered freely. O holder of the thunderbolt! be thou cognizant of our hymns, and cast thy weapon against the *Dasyu*, and increase the vigour and the fame of the *A'rya*."—*Rig Veda*, I. 103, 3.

"Indra protects his *A'rya* worshipper in wars. He who protects him on countless occasions protects him in all wars. He subdues for the benefit of (Aryan) men, the races who do not perform sacrifices. He flays the enemy of his dark skin, kills him, and reduces him to ashes. He burns those who are harmful and cruel." —*Rig Veda*, I. 130, 8.

"O Destroyer of foes! collect together the heads of these marauding troops, and crush them with thy wide foot! thy foot is wide.

"O Indra! destroy the power of these marauding troops. Throw them into the vile pit, the vast and vile pit!

"O Indra! thou hast destroyed three times fifty such troops! People extol thus thy deed; but it is nothing to thy prowess!"—*Rig Veda*, I. 133, 2-4.

"O Indra! Rishis still extol thy ancient deed of prowess. Thou hast destroyed many marauders to put an end to the war; thou hast stormed the towns of enemies who worship no gods; thou hast bent the weapons of enemies who worship no gods."—*Rig Veda*, I. 174, 7, 8.

It will be seen from hymns like these that the natural feeling of hostility between the *A'rya* or Aryan conquerors and the *Dasyu* aborigines was further embittered by difference in religion and religious rites. The Aryan believed in the "bright gods" of Nature, in the sky, the sun, the fire, and the storms; he sacrificed to them daily, and wherever he conquered, he carried with him his worship of Nature's deities and his cherished sacrificial rites. The dark-skinned *Dasyu* of the Punjab believed in no such gods, and performed no sacrifices, and this impiety and irreligion brought death and destruction on him, according to the belief of the sacrificing Hindu. Again and again the Hindu appealed to his martial deity, and confidently invoked his aid against men who were without faith and without rites.

Here and there we come across the names of wily barbarians, who continued the unequal combat with obstinacy, concealed themselves in fastnesses or in swamps, and harassed and plundered the Hindu settlers when they could.

"Kuyava gets scent of the wealth of others and plunders it. He lives in water and pollutes it. His wives bathe in the stream; may they be drowned in the depths of the Sifá river.

"Ayu lives in water in a secret fastness. He flourishes amidst the rise of waters. The rivers Anjasí, Kulisí, and Vírapatní protect him with their waters."—*Rig Veda*, I. 104, 3, 4.

"The fleet Krishna lived on the banks of the Ansumatí river with ten thousand troops. Indra of his own wisdom became cognizant of this loud-yelling chief. He destroyed the marauding host for the benefit of (Aryan) men.

"Indra said, 'I have seen the fleet Krishna. He is lurking in the hidden region near the Ansumatí, like the sun in a cloud. O Maruts! I desire you to engage in the fight and destroy him.'

"The fleet Krishna then appeared shining on the banks of the Ansumatí. Indra took Brihaspati as his ally, and destroyed the fleet and godless army."—*Rig Veda*, VIII. 96, 13–15.

How clearly these brief but realistic passages describe the running fight which was kept up by the retreating barbarians with the invincible conquerors. Renowned black warriors with their families and tribes concealed themselves in pathless woods, and in swamps and morasses made impregnable by the rise of rivers. From these unexplored wilds, they obtained information of the property and wealth and cattle of the white men living in fair villages; suddenly they proclaimed their presence by their uncouth yells, and in a moment the work of destruction was done, and the fleet plunderers disappeared as suddenly as they came. The colonists would not tamely bear such attacks; and often a raid by the aborigines was followed by a more determined and destructive expedition by the white settlers. Forests were explored and cleared; swamps and rivers were crossed; strong fastnesses were taken; and the offending chief and his "fleet and godless army" were at last hunted down and exterminated. It was by such reprisals that new forests were explored and brought under cultivation, river after river was crossed, settlement after settlement arose on the sites of swamps and woods,—and the great Aryan nation marched eastward until they fairly colonized the whole of the Punjab.

We know that the Spaniards owed their successes in America to a great extent to their horses, animals previously unknown to the American Indians, and regarded by them with a strange terror. It would seem that the war-horses of the Hindus inspired the black aborigines of India with equal terror. The following passage from a hymn to *Dadhikrá*, or the deified war-horse, will be read with interest :—

"As people shout and raise a cry after a thief who has purloined a garment, even so the enemies yell and shout at the sight of Dadhikrá! As birds make a noise at the sight of the hungry hawk in his descent, even so the enemies yell and shout at the sight of Dadhikrá, careering in quest of plunder, of food and cattle."

"Enemies fear Dadhikrá, who is radiant and destructive as a thunderbolt. When he beats back a thousand men, he becomes excited and uncontrollable in his strength."—*Rig Veda*, IV. 38, 5, 8.

Equally terrible to the aboriginal warriors was the war-drum of the Hindus, of which we find an account in hymn VI. 47. "The drum sounds loud to proclaim to all men (the hour of battle). Our leaders have mounted their steeds and have formed in order. O Indra! let our warriors who fight in chariots win victory."

In another remarkable hymn many of the weapons of war then used by the Hindus have been described, and the composition therefore has a historical value.

1. "When the battle is nigh, and the warrior marches in his armour, he appears like the cloud! Warrior, let not thy person be pierced; be victorious; let thy armour protect thee.

2. "We will win the cattle with the bow; we will win with the bow; we will conquer the fierce and proud enemy with the bow! May the bow foil the designs of the enemy! We will spread our conquests on all sides with the bow.

3. "The string of the bow when pulled approaches the ear of the archer. It whispers words of consolation to him, and it clasps the arrow with a sound, as a loving wife clasps her husband.

5. "The quiver is like the parent of many arrows, the arrows are like its children. It hangs, sounding, on the back of the warrior, it furnishes arrows in battle and conquers the enemy.

6. "The expert charioteer stands on his chariot and drives his horses wheresoever he will. The reins restrain the horses from behind. Sing of their glory!

7. "The horses raise the dust with their hoofs, and career over the fields with their chariots with loud neighings. They do not retreat but trample the marauding enemies under their hoofs."—*Rig Veda*, VI. 75.

Well might the uncivilized children of the soil retreat before these invincible conquerors who fought from their chariots, whose arrows were pointed with deer-horn or iron, and who were protected by their armour. We know from other passages that Hindu warriors also used helmets and shoulder-plates or shields, javelins, and battle-axes, and sharp-edged swords. Against troops so armed and led in order, the barbarians could offer little effective opposition. Occasionally there was war between hostile Hindu tribes; and a battle between two opposing Hindu armies, fighting with their chariots and horses, their armour, javelins and arrows, was not unlike those battles repeated day after day between the Greeks and the Trojans, of which we have such vivid accounts left to us in the pages of Homer.

For it should be remembered that the Hindu tribes, although constantly engaged in war with the aborigines, had nevertheless their petty jealousies and quarrels among themselves, which not unoften broke out into internecine wars. All the Hindu tribes of the Punjab were brave fighting nations; their kings were warriors and leaders of men; and jealousies and hostilities among rival tribes and rival chiefs were inevitable. Such wars became more frequent after the aborigines had been entirely subdued or expelled, and there was no common enemy to conquer. Tribe often rose against tribe, and state against state; and in one historically remarkable hymn we are told that no less than ten kings combined against the great king Sudás—the greatest hero of the Rig Veda—and Sudás was victorious over them all. The white-robed Tritsus or Vasishthas, who were the priests of Sudas's court, were proud of the ever memorable day of victory, and have celebrated it in verse which we must quote in full.

1. "O Leaders, Indra and Varuna! your worshippers, relying on your help, and seeking to win cattle, have marched eastwards with their weapons. Crush, Indra and Varuna, your enemies, whether *Dásas* or *A'ryas*, and defend Sudás with your protection.

2. "Where men raise their banners and meet in battle, where nothing seems to favour us, where the men look up to the sky and tremble, then, O Indra and Varuna! help us and speak to us.

3. "O Indra and Varuna! the ends of the earth seem to be lost, and the noise ascends to the skies. The troops of the enemy are approaching. O Indra and Varuna! who ever listen to our prayers, come near us with your protection.

4. "O Indra and Varuna! you pierced the yet unassailed Bheda and saved Sudás. You listened to the

prayers of the Tritsus. Their priestly vocation bore fruit in the hour of battle.

5. "O Indra and Varuna! the weapons of the enemy assail me in all directions; the foes assail me among marauding men. You are the owners of both kinds of wealth. Save us in the day of battle.

6. "Both parties invoked Indra and Varuna for wealth at the time of war. But in this battle you protected Sudás with the Tritsus who were attacked by ten kings.

7. "O Indra and Varuna! the ten kings who did not perform sacrifices were unable, though combined, to beat Sudás.

8. "You gave vigour, Indra and Varuna, to Sudás, when surrounded by ten chiefs; when the white-robed Tritsus, wearing braided hair, worshipped you with oblations and hymns.

9. "Indra destroys the enemy in battle; Varuna protects our pious rites. We invoke you with our praises. Bestow on us felicity, O Indra and Varuna.

10. "May Indra, Varuna, Mitra and Aryaman, grant us wealth and a spacious home. May the lustre of Aditi be harmless to us; we recite the praise of the divine Savitri."—*Rig Veda*, VII. 83.

CHAPTER III.

MANNERS AND CIVILIZATION.

WHEREVER the conquerors came, they cleared forests and introduced agriculture, which was the main industry of the ancient, as it is of modern Hindus. The very name, *A'rya*, by which the conquerors called themselves, is derived from a root which indicates tilling, and there is a beautiful short hymn on ploughing, which may be quoted as the oldest pastoral in the Aryan world.

1. "We will till this field with the Lord of the Field; may he nourish our horses; may he bless us thereby.

2. "O Lord of the Field! bestow on us sweet and pure and butter-like and delicious and copious rain, even as cows give us milk. May the Lords of Water bless us.

3. "May the crops be sweet unto us; may the skies and the rains and the firmament be full of sweetness; may the Lord of the Field be gracious to us. We will follow him unharmed by foes.

4. "Let the oxen work merrily; let the men work merrily; let the plough move on merrily. Fasten the traces merrily; ply the goad merrily.

5. "O Suna and Síra! accept this hymn. Moisten this earth with the rain you have created in the sky.

6. "O fortunate Sítá (Furrow)! proceed onwards, we pray unto thee. Do thou bestow on us wealth and an abundant crop.

7. "May Indra accept this Sítá; may Púshan lead

her onwards. May she be filled with water and yield us corn year after year.

8. "Let the ploughshares turn up the sod merrily; let the men follow the oxen merrily; let the god of rains moisten the earth with sweet rains. O Suna and Síra! bestow on us happiness."—*Rig Veda*, IV. 57.

This ancient agricultural song is marked by that simplicity and joyousness in active pursuits which mark all the most ancient effusions of the Hindus.

But cultivation on the Punjab on an extended scale was impossible, except by means of sinking wells and digging irrigation channels, and it is not remarkable that we find allusions to such contrivances in the songs of the Rig Vèda. Pasture land too was extensive; chiefs and leaders of men owned large herds of cattle, and warriors and poets prayed to the gods for increase of cattle and of wealth. Society was yet in its infancy, and was not yet marked by a hard and fast division into ranks; and we find in the Rig Veda, as in the pages of Homer, that the same chiefs who owned broad acres and pastured large herds of cattle in times of peace, distinguished themselves as leaders of men in times of war, and returned home after victories to worship their gods at their own firesides with copious libations, and with cakes or the flesh of victims. The earliest records and traditions of all Aryan nations point to this simple stage of civilization, when communities lived by agriculture and by pasture, when division into classes was little known, when all able-bodied men were warriors, and when great chiefs and leaders returned with their people to the plough after the war was over. Such is the picture of early Hindu life which the Rig Veda presents to us.

Barley and wheat were the principal produce of the field, and rice was as yet unknown. Animal food was however also largely indulged in, the bull and the ram were frequently sacrificed, and even the flesh of the horse was relished by the earlier Hindus, although in later times the sacrifice of the horse was reserved for imperial festivities only. The juice of the soma plant was a favourite drink, and was copiously used at sacrifices, and the poets of the Rig Veda go into ecstasies over the virtues and powers of this exhilarating beverage. In the end Soma was worshipped as a deity, as we shall see in the following chapter.

The simpler arts of civilized life were practised by the Punjab Hindus. Carpentry and weaving were well known, and considerable progress was made in the working of metals, of gold and silver and of iron. The weapons of war and various gold ornaments of which we find frequent mention show the progress made in these arts.

Of armour and helmets, javelins, swords and arrows, we have already made mention. Three thousand warriors covered with mail are spoken of in one remarkable verse (VI. 27, 6). In other places we are told of necklaces and bracelets and anklets, of golden plates for the breast, and of golden crowns for the head (V. 53 and 54, &c.). All these allusions show that a considerable advance was made by the Punjab Hindus in the working of metals.

Architecture too had made some advance, and there are allusions to "mansions with a thousand pillars". But we find no distinct mention of sculpture ; and the religion of the early Hindus, which was not idolatrous, did not foster that art.

The rules of social life were simple and patriarchal. The father of the family was its head, his sons and grandsons with their wives often lived under the same roof, and owned their lands and herds in common. The sacred fire was lighted in the house of every pious householder, the women of the family prepared the soma wine and other sacrificial requisites, and the benignant gods of the sky, firmament, and earth were invoked in simple hymns to be present at the sacrifices, and to bestow health and progeny and wealth on the sacrificers. Wives joined their husbands at these domestic sacrifices, and some beautiful hymns are still preserved to us which are said to have been composed by female worshippers.

There were no unhealthy restrictions upon Hindu women in those days, no rules to keep them secluded or debarred from their legitimate place in society. A girl generally selected her own husband, but her parents' wishes were for the most part respected. We have frequent allusions to careful and industrious wives who superintended the arrangements of the house, and, like the dawn, roused every one in the morning and sent him to his work. Girls who remained unmarried obtained a share in the paternal property. Widows could re-marry after the death of their husbands.

The ceremony of marriage was an appropriate one, and the promises which the bride and the bridegroom made were suitable to the occasion. We will quote a few verses from a remarkable hymn on this subject :—

(Address to the bride and bridegroom.) "Do ye remain here together; do not be separated. Enjoy food of various kinds; remain in your own home, and enjoy happiness in company of your children and grandchildren."

(The bride and bridegroom say.) "May Prajapati bestow on us children; may Aryaman keep us united till old age."

(Address to the bride.) "Enter, O bride! with auspicious signs the home of thy husband. Do good to our male servants and to our female servants, and to our cattle.

"Be thy eyes free from anger; minister to the happiness of thy husband; do good to our cattle. May thy mind be cheerful, may thy beauty be bright. Be the mother of heroic sons, and be devoted to the gods. Do good to our male servants and to our female servants, and to our cattle.

"O Indra! make this lady fortunate and the mother of worthy sons. Let ten sons be born of her, so that there may be eleven men with the husband."

(Address to the bride.) "May thou have influence over thy father-in-law and thy mother-in-law, and be as a queen over thy sister-in-law and brother-in-law."

(The bride and bridgroom say.) "May all the gods unite our hearts; may Mátarisvan and Dhátri and the goddess of speech unite us together."—*Rig Veda*, X. 85, 42 to 47.

These few verses give us a clear insight into the patriarchal family system of the olden days. The bride was a new-comer into her husband's family, and she was received with appropriate injunctions. The male servants, the female servants, and the very cattle were of the family, and the bride was asked to be kind and considerate and good to them all. Free from anger, and with a cheerful mind, she must not only minister to her husband's happiness, but be devoted to the gods worshipped in the family, and be kind to all its dependants She must extend her gentle influence over her husband's father and mother, she must keep under due control his brothers and sisters, and be the queen of the household. And thus she must remain, united to her husband until old age, the virtual mistress of a large and patriarchal family, and respected and honoured as Hindu women were honoured in ancient times.

Polygamy was allowed in ancient India as it was allowed among all ancient nations; but it was probably confined to kings and great chiefs only. The ordinary people were content with one wife. Sons inherited the property of their father, and in the absence of sons, the daughter's son or some other boy might be adopted.

Burial was probably the first form of funeral ceremony among ancient Hindus; but this was soon followed by cremation, and the ashes were then buried in the earth. A few verses from the funeral service will interest, and will show that the hopes of a future world cheered the last moments of a Hindu's life in ancient times, as they do at the present day.

"O thou deceased! proceed to the same place where our forefathers have gone, by the same path which they followed. The two kings Yama and Varuna are pleased with the offerings; go and meet them.

"Proceed to that happy heaven and mix with our forefathers. Meet Yama, and reap the fruits of thy virtuous deeds. Leave sin behind, enter thy home.

"O ye shades! leave this place, go away, move away. For the forefathers have prepared a place for the deceased. That place is beautiful with day, with sparkling waters and light. Yama assigns this place for the dead."—*Rig Veda*, X. 14, 7 to 9.

It is remarkable that there is no mention of a hell and its tortures in the Rig Veda.

CHAPTER IV.

RELIGION.

THE religion of the Hindus in the first or Vedic epoch was the worship of Nature leading up to Nature's God.

The hardy and enterprising conquerors of the Punjab were a warlike race with a capacity for active enjoyments, and an appreciation of all that was lovely and joyous in nature. They looked up to the beauteous and bright sky, and worshipped it under the name of *Dyu*, equivalent to the Greek *Zeus* and the first syllable of the Latin *Jupiter*. They also called the sky of day by the name of *Mitra*, corresponding to the Zend *Mithra*; and they called the sky of night *Varuna*, corresponding to the Greek *Ouranos*. These common names under which the sky-god was worshipped by the different Aryan nations of the ancient times prove that the sky was worshipped under these names by the primitive Aryans in their original home.

But while the Hindu Aryans of the Punjab continued to worship the ancient sky-god under the ancient names of Dyu, Mitra, and Varuna, they paid special homage to the *sky that rains*, which they called *Indra*. For in India the rise of rivers and the luxuriance of crops depend on the rain-giving sky; and in course of time Indra became the most prominent deity in the Hindu pantheon. He was conceived as a warlike deity, battling with the clouds, called Vritra, to obtain copious torrents of rain for man, and fighting with the demons of darkness, called Panis, to restore to the world the light of the morning. The

Maruts or storm-gods were supposed to help Indra in his contest with the reluctant clouds, for in India the first showers of the rainy season are often attended with storms and thunder. And the deity, at once so beneficent and so warlike, was naturally a favourite with the martial and conquering Hindus; and as we have seen before, they constantly invoked him to lead them against the retreating barbarians, and to bestow on the conquerors new lands and wealth, cattle and progeny.

It will help us to enter into the spirit of the warlike and simple Hindu worshippers of the olden times if we read some verses describing the battles of Indra with the cloud.

1. "We sing the heroic deeds which were done by Indra the thunderer. He destroyed Ahi (clouds), and caused rains to descend, and opened out the paths for the mountain streams to roll.

2. "Indra slew Ahi resting on the mountains; Tvashtri had made the far-reaching thunderbolt for him. Water in torrents flowed towards the sea, as cows run eagerly towards their calves.

3. "Impetuous as a bull, Indra quaffed the soma juice; he drank the soma libations offered in the three sacrifices. He then took the thunderbolt, and thereby slew the eldest of the Ahis.

4. "When you killed the eldest of the Ahis, you destroyed the contrivances of the artful contrivers. You cleared the sun and the morning and the sky, and left no enemies behind.

5. "Indra with his all-destructive thunderbolt slew the darkling Vritra (clouds) and lopped his limbs. Ahi now lies touching the earth like the trunk of a tree felled by the axe.

8. "Glad waters are bounding over the prostrate body as rivers flow over fallen banks. Vritra when alive had

withheld the waters by his power, Ahi now lies prostrate under the waters."—*Rig Veda*, I. 32.

Let us contrast with this the following verses addressed to Varuna the sky-god of righteousness, and we shall perceive how the ancient Hindus worshipped the sky in its different aspects under different names, now as the Lord of tempests and of rain, now as the Lord of mercy.

3. "O Varuna! with an anxious heart I ask thee about my sins. I have gone to learned men to make the inquiry; the sages have all said to me, 'Varuna is displeased with thee'.

4. "O Varuna! for what deed of mine dost thou wish to destroy thy friend, thy worshipper? O thou of irresistible power, declare it to me, so that I may quickly bend in adoration and come to thee.

5. "O Varuna! deliver us from the sins of our fathers. Deliver us from the sins committed in our person. O royal Varuna! deliver Vasishtha like a calf from its tether, like a thief who has feasted on a stolen animal.

6. "O Varuna! all this sin is not wilfully committed by us. Error or wine, anger or dice, or even thoughtlessness has begotten sin. Even an elder brother leads his younger astray. Sin is begotten even in our dreams.

7. "Freed from sins, I will serve as a slave the god Varuna, who fulfils our wishes and supports us. We are ignorant; may the *A'rya* god bestow on us knowledge. May the wise deity accept our prayer and bestow on us wealth."—*Rig Veda*, VII. 86.

Next to the sky, the sun was the most prominent object of the worship of the ancient Hindus. *Aditi* was the limitless light of sky, and her sons, the *A'dityas*, were the suns of the different months of the year. *Súrya*, answering to the Greek Helios, the Latin Sol, and the Teuton Tyr, was, however, the most popular name by which the sun was worshipped. *Savitri* is another name of the same deity, and the sacred hymn, the Gáyatrí, which is still repeated every morning by pious Brahmans all over India, as the first act of their daily devotions, is a verse addressed to their deity. It runs thus in translation:—

"We meditate on the desirable light of the divine Savitri who influences our pious rites."—*Rig Veda*, III. 62, 10.

Viewed in other aspects the sun had other names. Pasture was still extensively followed by the Punjab Hindus as a means of living, and the simple shepherds looked on the sun as their guide and protector in all their migrations, and called him *Púshan.*

1. "O Púshan! help us to finish our journey, and remove all dangers. O son of the cloud! do thou march before us.

2. "O Púshan! do thou remove from our path him who would lead us astray, who strikes and plunders and does wrong.

3. "Do thou drive away that wily robber who intercepts journeys.

7. "Lead us so that enemies who intercept may not harm us; lead us by easy and pleasant paths. O Púshan! devise means for our safety on this journey.

8. "Lead us to pleasant tracks covered with green grass; may there not be excessive heat by the way. O Púshan! devise means for our safety on this journey." —*Rig Veda*, I. 42.

One more name of the sun it is necessary to mention. *Vishnu*, which in later Hindu mythology has become a name of the Supreme Preserver of all beings, was a name of the sun in the Vedic age. The rising sun, the sun at zenith, and the setting sun were considered the three steps of Vishnu striding across limitless space.

Fire or *Agni* was an object of worship. No sacrifice to the gods could be performed without libations or offerings to the fire, and Agni was therefore considered to be the priest among the gods. But Agni is not only the terrestrial fire in the Rig Veda; he is also the fire of the lightning and the sun, and his abode was in heaven. The early sages Bhrigus discovered him there, and Atharvan and Angiras, the first sacrificers, installed him in this world as the protector of men.

Váyu, or the wind, is sometimes invoked in the Rig Veda. The *Maruts*, or storm-gods, are oftener invoked, as we have seen before, and are considered the helpers of Indra in obtaining rain for the benefit of man. *Rudra*, the loud-sounding father of the Maruts, is the Thunder, and in later Hindu mythology this name has been appropriately chosen for the Supreme Destroyer of all living beings.

We have said that Agni, or fire, received special homage because he was necessary for all sacrifice. The libation of soma juice was similarly regarded sacred, and *Soma* was worshipped as a deity. Similarly, the prayer which accompanied the libations or offerings was also regarded as a deity, and was called *Brahmanaspati*. In later Hindu mythology, Brahman is selected as the name of the Supreme Creator of all living beings.

We have now enumerated the most important gods of the Vedic pantheon, but it is necessary to add a word about the twin-gods of the Rig Veda, Morning and Evening. Light and Darkness naturally suggested to the early Aryans the idea of twin gods. The sky (Vivasvat) is the father, and the Dawn (Saranyu) is the mother of the twin *Asvins*, and the legend goes on to say that Saranyu ran away from Vivasvat before she gave birth to the twins. We have the same legend in Greek mythology; and Erinnys (answering philologically to Saranyu) ran away from her lover, and gave birth to Areion and Despoina. The original idea is that the ruddy nymph (Dawn and Gloaming) disappears, and gives birth to Light and to Darkness.

But whatever the original conception may have been, the Asvins have lost their primitive character in the Rig Veda, and have simply become physician gods, healers of the sick and the wounded, tending mortals with kindness. Similarly the twins, *Yama* and his sister *Yamí* (children of the same parents, Sky and Dawn, and originally implying Light and Darkness), have also acquired a different character in the Rig Veda. Of Yamí we hear little, but Yama is the ruler of the future world, the beneficent king of the departed. Clothed in a glorious body, the virtuous live in the future life by the side of Yama, in the realms of light and sparkling waters. Two short extracts from hymns to Yama and to Soma respectively, will illustrate the idea of future life and future felicity which the Hindus of the Vedic age entertained.

1. "Worship Yama, the son of Vivasvat, with offerings. All men go to him. He takes men of virtuous deeds to the realm of happiness. He clears the way for many.

2. "Yama first discovered the path for us. That path will not be destroyed again. All living beings will, according to their acts, follow by the path by which our forefathers have gone."—*Rig Veda*, X. 14.

7. "Flowing Soma! take me to that immortal and imperishable abode where light dwells eternal, and which is in heaven. Flow, Soma! for Indra.

8. "Take me where Yama is king, where are the gates of heaven, and where mighty rivers flow. Take me there and make me immortal. Flow, Soma! for Indra.

9. "Take me where is the third heaven, where is the third realm of light above the sky, and where one can

wander at his will. Take me there, and make me immortal. Flow, Soma! for Indra.

10. "Take me where every desire is satiated, where Pradhma has his abode, where there is food and contentment. Take me there and make me immortal. Flow, Soma! for Indra.

11. "Take me where there are pleasures and joys and delights, and where every desire of the anxious heart is satiated. Take me there, and make me immortal. Flow, Soma! for Indra."—*Rig Veda*, XI. 113.

The deities named above are the most important gods of the Rig Veda. Of goddesses there are only two who have any marked character or individuality, viz., *Ushas* or Dawn and *Sarasvatî* the river-goddess.

There is no lovelier conception in the Rig Veda than that of the Dawn, and there are no fresher or more beauteous passages in the lyrical poetry of the ancient world than some of the hymns dedicated to Ushas. She is described as the far-extending, many-tinted, brilliant Dawn, whose abode is unknown. She harnesses her chariots from afar and comes in radiance and glory. She is the young, the white-robed daughter of the sky, the queen of all earthly treasures. She is like the careful mistress of the house who rouses every one from his slumbers and sends him to his work. And yet she is radiant as a bride decorated by her mother for the auspicious ceremony, and displaying her charms to the view.* Such are the fond epithets and beautiful similes with which the Hindu Aryans greeted the fresh and lovely mornings of a tropical sky.

It is remarkable that the Hellenic Aryans of the time of Homer regarded the lovely Eos with much the same feeling of poetic fondness. But the mystery is explained when we learn that Eos is the same name as Ushas, and

* *Rig Veda*, I. 30, 21; I. 48, 7; I. 113, 7; I. 124, 4; I. 123, 11.

that the other Greek names of the Dawn correspond philologically to Hindu names of the same deity,* and there can be little doubt, therefore, that the Hindu and the Hellenic Aryans alike derived their conceptions and their names of the Dawn-goddess from the primitive Aryans.

This remark does not apply in the case of Sarasvatí, who is purely a Hindu goddess. Sarasvatí is the name of a river in the Punjab,† deemed to be holy because of the religious rites which were performed on its banks and the sacred hymns uttered there. By a natural development of ideas she came to be considered the goddess of those hymns or the goddess of speech, in which character she is worshipped in India to the present day.

From the foregoing account the reader will perceive that there was an essential difference between the Hindu gods of the Vedic age and the Greek gods of the Homeric age. The Hindu conceptions go nearer to the original Nature-worship of the primitive Aryans, even as the Sanscrit language is nearer and closer than the Greek to the original Aryan tongue. Among the Greeks of the Homeric age, the gods and goddesses have already attained a marked individuality; their history, their character, their deeds, engage our attention; their connection with the powers and manifestations of Nature almost escapes us. The Hindu gods of the Vedic age, on the contrary, are obviously still Nature's powers and manifestations; they have scarcely any other character or history. We can more clearly identify Dyu with the sky than Zeus, and Ahaná and Dahaná are more obviously and manifestly the Dawn than Athena and Daphne. The Hindu conceptions are more ancient, more archaic, more true to their original sources. The Greek conceptions

* Argynoris is Arjuni of the Veda, Daphne is Dahaná, Athena is Ahaná, Erinnys is Saranyu, &c.

† Some identify the Sarasvatí with the river Indus itself.

are more developed, and have passed farther from the domain of Nature-worship to that of Polytheism.

It is probably owing to this difference that the Hindus attained to a conception of the one supreme God sooner than the Greeks. It was an easy step from the worship of natural powers to the conception of Nature's God; but it was not easy for the Greeks, who had already invested their gods with distinct characters and histories, to set them aside and rise to the conception of one God. The Greeks of the Homeric age failed, therefore, to rise to the worship of the Supreme Deity, which the Hindus succeeded in doing even in the Vedic Age.

In some of the latest hymns of the Rig Veda we find that the worshipper correctly interpreted the names of the different gods as only different names of the same great Power, the Father of all, the Creator of all.

1. "The all-wise Father saw clearly, and after due reflection created the sky and the earth in their watery form, and touching each other. When their boundaries were stretched afar, then the sky and the earth became separated.

2. "The Creator of all is great; he creates and supports all; he is above all, and sees all; he is beyond the seat of the seven Rishis. So the wise men say, and the wise men obtain fulfilment of their desires.

3. "He who has given life, he who is the Creator, he who knows all the places in this universe,—*he is one, although he bears the names of many gods.* Other beings wish to know him."—*Rig Veda*, X. 82.

This is the earliest indication of Hindu monotheism, that monotheism which has continued to be the true religion of the Hindus for over three thousand years, in spite of the legends and allegories and "the names of many gods" with which the popular mind has been fed from age to age.

One more extract, a sublime hymn to the same supreme God, will enable us to understand this the earliest phase of Hindu monotheism.

1. "In the beginning the Golden Child existed. He was the Lord of all from his birth. He placed this earth and sky in their proper places. Whom shall we worship with offerings?

2. "Him who has given life and strength, whose will is obeyed by all gods, whose shadow is immortality, and whose slave is Death. Whom shall we worship with offerings?

3. "Him who by his power is the sole King of all the living beings that see and move; him who is the Lord of all bipeds and quadrupeds. Whom shall we worship with offerings?

4. "Him by whose power these shadowy mountains have been made, and whose creations are this earth and its oceans; him whose arms are these quarters of space. Whom shall we worship with offerings?

5. "Him who has fixed in their places this sky and this earth; him who has established the heavens and the highest heaven; him who has measured the firmament. Whom shall we worship with offerings?

6. "Him by whom the sounding sky and earth have been fixed and expanded; him whom the resplendent sky and earth own as Almighty; him by whose support the sun rises and gains lustre. Whom shall we worship with offerings?"—*Rig Veda*, X. 121.

It will thus be seen that the religion of the sturdy conquerors of the Punjab was a progressive religion, leading from Nature up to Nature's God. We see the entire journey of the human mind in the Rig Veda—a work unique in the world for this reason—from the simple, child-like admiration of the ruddy dawn or the breaking storm, to the sublime effort to grasp the mysteries of creation and its great Creator.

While a few of the advanced spirits of the age rose to this height, the nation still continued to invoke their beloved gods, and poured libations and offered cakes to them with their prayers. There were no temples and no hereditary priests. Each pious householder, each patriarch of his family, lighted the sacrificial fire in his own home, poured the soma juice in libations, and prayed to the gods for health and crops, for cattle and progeny.

Great kings and chiefs, however, performed their religious sacrifices with ostentatious prodigality, and families of priests were supported by such chiefs and presided at all royal observances. In course of time such families, who followed the same vocation from generation to generation, became known for their skill in composing or reciting hymns and performing rites. Different collections of hymns were preserved in such families, handed down from father to son, and preserved by memory alone, and it is to this pious custom that the Aryan world owes the preservation of the earliest of Aryan compositions now extant, *i.e.*, the hymns of the Rig Veda.

But although certain families followed the vocation of priests from father to son, and were therefore rewarded by princes and respected by the people, there was no hereditary distinction yet between the priest and the people, and the caste system of India was unknown in the Vedic Age. The only insuperable distinction which existed in that age was between the conquerors and the conquered, the Hindus and the Aborigines, the *A'ryans* and the *Dasyus*, as they are styled in the Rig Veda. Among the Aryan Hindus themselves no such distinction was yet known, and the patriarchs and leaders of the Punjab Hindus composed their hymns, fought their battles, and ploughed their fields before the castes of the Brahmans, Kshatriyas, and Vaisyas were formed.

EPOCH II.—EPIC AGE.

HINDU KINGDOMS ON THE GANGES.
B.C. 1400-1000.

CHAPTER I.

KURUS AND PANCHÁLAS.

WHEN the Hindus had conquered and settled in the wide extent of country from the Indus to the Sutlej and the Sarasvati, they were not long in sending out colonies farther east, towards the Ganges. The stream of emigrants and colonists increased from age to age, until the banks of the Ganges were studded with fair villages and towns surpassing in wealth and civilization those of the mother-land, Punjab. In the Rig Veda the home of the Hindus is the Punjab, and the allusions to the distant shores of the Ganges are rare. In the literature of the next succeeding epoch, which we may call the Epic Age, the shores of the Ganges are the home of most renowned and civilized Hindu kingdoms; the mother-country of the Punjab is already thrown into the shade.

Among the colonists who emigrated from the Punjab to the banks of the Ganges, the Kurus and the Panchálas were not the least distinguished. The Kurus were originally known under the name of Bháratas, and had figured in the wars of Sudás, of which we have spoken in a preceding chapter. Numbers of them left their home and migrated eastwards, until, in the fourteenth century before Christ, they had founded a flourishing kingdom on the upper course of the Ganges. The nation was still known as the Bhảratas, or under the newer name of Kurus, from the name of their kings, and they built their capital at Hastinápura, on the Ganges.

The Panchálas also came from the Punjab. The Punjab Hindus, or some tribes among them, are called in the Rig Veda, Pancha Jana or Pancha Krishti, *i.e.*, the "five tribes", or the "five agricultural races", and it is probable that the descendants of these races colonized the shores of the Ganges under the name of the Panchálas or "five tribes". They settled immediately to the south of the Bhảratas or Kurus, and had founded a powerful kingdom there by the fourteenth century before Christ, and called their capital Kámpilya.

Other nations from the Punjab also came and settled on the course of the Upper Ganges and the Jumna, among whom the Yadavas, the Matsyas, and the Surasenas were the most important. They are known to us from the share which they took in the great war, of which we will speak farther on.

The Kurus and the Panchálas lived in peace and friendly rivalry for a long time, and developed a civilization surpassing that of their sturdy and rough ancestors in the Punjab. Kings had polished courts, and delighted in assembling the wise and the learned of the age, who held controversies on morals, religion, and philosophy. Priests rejoiced in the performance of elaborate sacrifices, lasting for days, or weeks, or years, for the edification of monarchs; and were rewarded according to their learning and their merits. Learned men received pupils for education, and all Aryan Hindus made over their children at an early age to the charge of such teachers or *Gurus*.

Every boy lived with his Guru for years together, served him in a menial capacity, begged alms for his support, tended his flocks, swept his house, and acquired from him from day to day, and from year to year, the sacred knowledge of the Vedas and of other branches of learning which were the cherished heritage of the ancient Hindus. After leaving the Guru, and rewarding him handsomely, some young men prosecuted their studies further in *Parishads*, answering to modern universities, where a number of teachers bestowed instruction in different subjects; and after the completion of their education they returned to their homes, married, and settled down as householders.

The sacrificial fire was lighted on the occasion of the marriage, and every pious Hindu kept up the fire in his house, and offered to it libations and offerings as required by his religion. The hymns of the Veda were still uttered at the sacrifices, and the same religion, the same customs and rites, the same common language, prevailed among the different Hindu communities which flourished on the Ganges and the Jumna over three thousand years ago.

Indeed, as we study the state of the Hindu races of this epoch, each race forming a separate community and a kingdom of its own, and all races rejoicing in the same language, the same religion, and the same common civilization and manners, we are strongly reminded of the Greek cities which flourished side by side before the Peloponnesian war. Rivalries, and even hostilities, were as common among the Hindu races as among the Greek cities, while communications of a more friendly nature kept up their mutual relations. The schools of learning of the different races vied with each other, and the Parishads of the Kurus and the Panchálas attracted large numbers of students from other nations. In the midst of all this friendly rivalry, the Hindu tribes never relaxed their preparations for war. Princes of the royal houses and of the military classes were early trained in arms as in arts, and were familiar with the bow and the arrow, the sword, the javelin, and the *chakra* or quoit. Jealousies among the different races broke out not unoften into open hostilities; and, as if to complete the parallel between the Indian states and the Greek cities, there was a great and sanguinary war in the thirteenth century before Christ, answering to the Peloponnesian war of Greece, in which all the known Hindu tribes of Northern India joined, and which ended in great carnage and slaughter.

This war forms the subject of the great Hindu epic known as the *Mahábhárata*; and, as might be expected, the real causes and events of the struggle are lost in fables and myths. The war was waged between the great races, the Kurus or Bháratas and the Panchálas, and the name of the epic signifies "the Great Bharata".

Neither the Kurus nor the Panchálas, however, are the heroes of the epic as it has come down to us. The Pancha Pándava, or the five sons of Pándu, are the heroes, and their common wife, the daughter of the king of the Panchálas, is the heroine. The origin of this fable of the five Pándavas and of their common wife, which now forms the central story of the Hindu epic, has given rise to much discussion, into which it it needless to enter. It is certain that this central story is a myth.

The most probable supposition is that the Pándavas were a distinct race, who helped or led the Panchálas in the war; that the race is metaphorically represented in the epic as five brothers, and that their alliance with the Panchálas is metaphorically represented as their marrying a maiden of the Panchála house. Polyandry was unknown to the Hindus of ancient India, as it is to the Hindus of the present day.

It has also been supposed that at an age subsequent to the time of the war, and when kings of the Pándava race wielded supreme power, the epic was first compiled from ballads, legends, or recollections relating to the great contest. Naturally, therefore, the supposed forefathers of the ruling race were represented as the heroes of the strife; and although belonging to a distinct race, they were represented as cousins of the Kuru princes, so that later generations might not look upon them as usurpers.

From what has been stated above, it is apparent that we shall seek in vain in the epic for the real incidents of the war. But, nevertheless, it throws much light on the age of which we are now speaking, and no history of India, therefore, is complete without some account, however brief, of the war, even as disguised in the existing epic.

A king of the Kurus left two sons, of whom Dhritaráshtra, the elder, was blind, and Pándu, the younger, ascended the throne of Hastinápura. Pándu died, leaving five sons, the heroes of the epic, and jealousies and quarrels soon arose between them and the hundred sons of their uncle, Dhritaráshtra.

The five sons of Pándu were trained in arms by their preceptor, Drona. The eldest, Yudhishthira, never became much of a warrior, but was versed in the religious lore of the age, and is the most righteous character in the epic. Bhíma, the second, was known for his great size and giant strength, and is the Hercules of the poem. Arjuna, the third, is the real hero of the epic, and excelled all in the skill of arms. Nakula, the fourth, learned to tame wild horses, and Sahadeva, the fifth, became proficient in astronomy. These brothers incurred the jealousy and hatred of their cousins from their youth up.

At last the day came for a public exhibition of the skill which the princes had acquired in the use of arms. A spacious area was enclosed. Nobles and ladies sat around to watch the tournament. The blind Dhritaráshtra was led to his seat, and foremost among the ladies were his queen and the widow of Pándu, and the population of Kuru-land flocked around to see and admire the skill of their beloved princes.

There were fights with swords and clubs, and skill in archery was tried by severe tests. Arjuna distinguished himself above all the rest, and, amidst the ringing cheers of the assembled multitude, concluded his wonderful feats by doing obeisance to the venerable preceptor, Drona.

The dark cloud of jealousy lowered on the brow of the sons of Dhritaráshtra, and when the time came for the election of a king, they rebelled against Pándu's eldest son ascending his father's throne. The just and aged Dhritaráshtra had to yield; his sons obtained the royal power, and the five Pándavas were sent into exile.

Heralds now went through the different Hindu states, announcing that the daughter of the king of the Panchálas would select a husband by the ancient *Swayamvara* rite; in other words, she would herself choose her lord from among the most skilful warriors of the time. A heavy bow of great size was to be wielded, and an arrow was to be sent through a whirling *chakra* or quoit into the eye of a golden fish set high on a pole. The happy warrior who did this would win the princess.

Princes and warriors flocked to Kámpilya, the capital of the Panchálas. The princess appeared with her brother among the assembled nobles, with the garland which she was to bestow on the victor of the day. Many tried to wield the bow, but in vain. An unknown warrior then stepped forward, drew the bow, and shot the arrow into the eye of the golden fish. Murmurs of discontent arose, like the sound of troubled waters, from the ranks of the warriors at the success of this unknown archer; but the latter threw off his disguise, and proclaimed himself the proud, the exiled Arjuna.

Then follows the strange myth that the five brothers went to their mother and said that a great prize had been won. Their mother, not knowing what the prize was, told her sons to share it among them; and as a mother's mandate cannot be disregarded, the five Pándavas wedded the princess as their common wife. The Pándavas were now allied with the Panchálas, and their claim to their father's throne could no longer be gainsaid. A division was therefore made of the kingdom to prevent a war. The division was, however, unequal. Hastinápura and the best portion of Kuru-land fell to the share of the sons of Dhritaráshtra. Forest lands on the Jumna were given to the Pándavas, where they cleared the woods, and built their new capital of Indraprastha, on the site of modern Delhi.

From this new capital the Pándavas spread their conquests far and wide, and Yudhishthira invited the princes of all neighbouring countries, including his kinsmen of Hastinápura, to attend the great coronation ceremony. A quarrel arose in the assembly between Sisupála, king of the Chedis, and Krishna of the Yadava race, and the latter killed Sisupála on the spot. Thenceforward Krishna remained a staunch ally of the Pándavas; and in the epic in its present form he is represented as a deity who had assumed human form in order to help the Pándavas to their rights.

But the newly crowned king was not long to enjoy his kingdom. With all his righteousness, Yudhishthira had a weakness for gambling, and the eldest son of Dhritaráshtra challenged him to a game. Kingdom, wealth, himself and his brothers, and even his wife, were staked by Yudhishthira and lost, and behold now the five brothers and their wife the slaves of their rivals! That proud princess was dragged by the hair to the assembly and insulted, and bloodshed was imminent, when the old Dhritaráshtra was led into the room and stopped the tumult. It was decided that the Pándavas had lost their kingdom, but should not be slaves. They agreed to go into exile for twelve years, after which they should remain concealed for a year. If the sons of Dhritaráshtra failed to discover them within this last year, they would get their kingdom back.

Thus the Pándavas went again into exile, and, after twelve years of wandering, took service in disguise in the thirteenth year under the king of Viráta. Their wife also took service in the same court as the queen's handmaid. A difficulty arose. The queen's brother became enamoured of the handmaid and insulted her. Bhíma interfered and killed the lover in secret.

Cattle-lifting was not uncommon among the princes of those days, and the princes of Hastinápura carried away some cattle from Viráta. Arjuna, then in the service of Viráta, could not stand this; he put on his armour and recovered the cattle, but was discovered. The point whether the year of secret exile had quite expired was never settled, and thus the poet leaves undecided the question of the justice of the war which followed.

The Pándavas now made themselves known and claimed back their kingdom. The claim was refused, and both parties prepared for a war, the like of which had not been witnessed in India. All the Hindu nations joined one side or the other, and a great battle was fought in the plains of Kurukshetra, north of Delhi, which lasted for eighteen days. The story of this battle, with its endless episodes, need not detain us. All the great Kuru warriors and princes were killed, and Yudhishthira waded through blood to the ancient throne of Kuru-land.

Such is the main outline of the plot of the Mahábhárata,

and the story throws much light on the manners of the Hindus of the Epic Age. We find how young princes were early trained in arms, how they rejoiced in tilts and tournaments in their own fashion, how ladies came out in public and witnessed the prowess of their sons, brothers, or husbands. Girls were married at a proper age, and youthful princesses, famed for their beauty, often selected their lords from the assembled warriors; and jealousies among kings and nations broke out into sanguinary wars, but the bitterness of feuds was restrained by strict laws of chivalry.

We also learn from the epic that the Gangetic Hindus were more civilized than their sturdy forefathers of the Punjab. Kings ruled over larger countries, manners were more polished, the sphere of knowledge was more extended. Religious rites were also more elaborate, social rules were more highly developed, and the science of war itself was more fully organized. But, nevertheless, the stubborn valour and determination of Vedic warriors break through the more polished manners of the Epic Age, and the proud colonist races who founded the great and civilized kingdoms on the banks of the Ganges had not yet lost the vigour of national life which had animated their ruder forefathers in the Punjab.

CHAPTER II.

KOSALAS, VIDEHAS, AND KÁSÍS.

WHILE the Kurus and the Panchálas, and other less known races, remained in lands adjoining the upper course of the Ganges, other Aryan tribes penetrated farther eastwards, and settled lower down the same river. The Kosalas were among the most distinguished of these colonists. Their ancestors are said to have fought in the wars of Sudas in the Punjab, and they now marched eastwards with their priests, the Tritsus or Vasishthas, and founded a powerful and extensive kingdom, stretching from the Ganges as far east as the Gandak river; and they brought with them the same religion and institutions, the language, learning, and arts, which were the common heritage of all Aryan Hindus. Ayodhyá or Oudh was their capital town.

A still more celebrated tribe, the Videhas, marched farther eastwards, crossed the Gandak river, and settled in the country now known as Tirhút, to the north of the Ganges. Their earliest traditions narrate that their ancestor, Madhava Videha, came from the banks of the Sarasvatí in the Punjab, with his priest Gautama, and, after travelling through various lands and crossing many rivers, came to the country of Tirhút. The hero then inquired, "Where am I to abide?" "To the east of this (Gandak river) be thy abode," replied the god Agni, and the Videha thereupon settled in Tirhút. The country was marshy and uncultivated at that time, but the industrious colonists drained swamps, burnt down forests, extended the limits of cultivation, and founded their capital of Mithilá.

A third distinguished nation, the Kásís, also came from the west and settled on the banks of the Ganges, and founded their far-famed capital, still known as Kási or Benáres, the holiest city in India.

It may be easily imagined that these colonist nations did not neglect the religion and the religious rites of their forefathers. Indeed, colonists in all parts of the world cherish the institutions of their mother-land with an almost superstitious regard, and the Hindu colonists in the Gangetic valley accordingly came to attach a far greater importance to the forms and rites of Hindu worship than their ancestors had done in the Punjab. It was these rites that distinguished them from the outer barbarians, and that connected them with the earliest days of their glorious conquests in India. Coming to new lands, and surrounded by new and uncivilized aboriginal races, they adhered closely and steadfastly to those forms and institutions which marked them as Aryans, and which they cherished as their sacred inheritance. And as the distance of their new settlements from the Punjab increased with every fresh conquest, and as centuries divided them from the days of their early civilization and religion, they clung to the forms of that religion and civilization with an increasing veneration and regard, until the *forms* and *rites* concealed the substance and became their new *religion.*

It is necessary to clearly comprehend these facts in the history of the early Hindus in order to understand the change which now came over their manners. The same deities that were worshipped in the Punjab were worshipped by the Gangetic Hindus, and the same prayers of the Veda were uttered. But the simple forms of sacrifice now became more elaborate and cumbrous; every little rite was invested with a hidden meaning, every necessary act connected with worship came to be regarded as sacred, and the spirit of the religion of the Vedas was lost in the performance of elaborate sacrifices which took days and months and years. Kings now ruled over larger and richer and more populous kingdoms than the warrior chiefs of the Punjab, and had therefore both the power and the inclination for more ostentatious forms of sacrifice. Priests, too, now formed themselves into a separate class or caste, and had an interest therefore in making the performance of sacrifices difficult, and even impracticable, for others. And the people of the Lower Gangetic regions, living in a genial but enervating climate, lost something of the sturdiness of their forefathers, and became more submissive and luxurious, more addicted to ostentatious display and elaborate forms. Thus a great change came almost imperceptibly over the spirit of Hindu religion. In the Vedic Age men worshipped with gratitude and wonder the great and beneficent manifestations and powers of nature, offered prayers and food and libations to the fire, to express their devotion and their friendliness to the gods. In the Epic Age men's eyes were gradually withdrawn from the objects of worship, and the mere forms and ceremonials of the sacrifice, the performance of every petty rite in the proper way and at the proper time, and the utterance of every word with the proper accent, engrossed the attention of priests and people, and took the place of religion itself.

The hymns of the Vedas were classified and arranged for the purpose for which they were now required. The entire body of the hymns was known as the *Rig Veda.* By an ancient custom some of these hymns were chanted in some forms of sacrifice, and a collection of these select hymns, set to music, was called the *Sáma Veda.* Again, special sacrificial formulas were required for the use of the officiating priests, and these formulas were separately collected and known as the *Yajur Veda*. These were the three Vedas recognized by the Gangetic Hindus, but a later composition known as the *Atharva Veda* was afterwards recognized as the fourth Veda. The Vedas were thus separately compiled early in the Epic Age, before the Kuru-Panchála war.

But the religious literature of this age does not consist of the Vedas alone. As has often occurred in other countries and in other ages, dogmatic explanations and commentaries soon came to acquire a greater importance than the texts themselves. Each Veda has a number of such commentaries, and these commentaries, or *Bráhmanas*, as they are called, form the most voluminous portion of the literature of this age. They are generally uninteresting and vapid.

But a healthy reaction was at hand. It would seem that earnest and thoughtful kings in this period felt some impatience at this display of priestly erudition and pedantry, and, while still conforming to the rites laid down by the priests, started healthier speculations as to the destination of the human soul and the nature of the Universal Being. Nothing in the history of ancient India is more curious than this ancient rivalry between kings and priests at this remote age; and nothing is more fresh and life-giving than the earnest speculations which arose from this rivalry, and which are known as the *Upanishads*.

The kings of the Videhas and the Kásís took a leading part in starting these pious inquiries. Janaka, king of the Videhas, was the most saintly character of the age, and was deeply versed in its pious learning. His court was crowded by the learned and the wise. His great priest, Yájnavalkya, compiled a new edition of the Yajur Veda, which is known as the White Yajur Veda, and also an elaborate commentary or Bráhmana of this Veda. But Yájnavalkya was not the only honoured priest in Janaka's court. All learned men from the different Gangetic kingdoms sought the bounty of the king of the Videhas, and none sought it in vain. Even Ajátasatru, the king of the Kásís, himself a celebrated patron of learning, exclaimed in despair, "Verily, all people run away, saying, Janaka is our patron."

The names of Janaka and Ajátasatru are preserved in the Upanishads for the part they took in starting earnest speculations and pious inquiries. The Upanishads will form the subject of a future chapter, but it is necessary to quote one or two short legends here to show how these learned and saintly kings explained to the self-sufficient priests of the time the true scope and object of religion.

Janaka of Videha, we are told, once met three priests, one of whom was his court priest, Yájnavalkya. A discussion ensued, and the three priests were humiliated and sad, until Yájnavalkya followed the king in his car and learnt the truth from him.

Similarly, once upon a time a boastful priest, Báláki, challenged Ajátasatru, king of the Kásís, to a discussion. In the course of the dispute, however, the priest was defeated and remained silent and sad. Ajátasatru then said, "Thus far do you know, O Báláki!" "Thus far only," replied Báláki. "O Báláki!" then explained the royal sage, "he who is the maker of all those, he of whom all this is the work, he (God) alone should be known."

Similarly, a Brahman or priest, Svetaketu, came to an assembly of the Panchálas, and there had a discussion with Jaivali, a Kshatriya or king. The Brahman was defeated, and came sad and sorrowful to the Kshatriya to learn the truth. The king explained the truth, and said, "This knowledge did not go to any Brahman before you, and therefore this teaching belonged in all the worlds to the Kshatriya (royal) class alone."

Such are some of the legends which have been handed down to us, indicating faintly but unmistakably the rivalry which raged between the priestly and military classes just when these classes were forming into separate castes, and they also disclose to us the share which the royal caste took in originating or promoting the inquiries which are preserved to us in the Upanishads, and which have formed the basis of Hindu monotheism to the present day. Janaka was one of these earnest inquirers, and as such his name is entitled to respect.

But the mass of the Hindus of the present day remember Janaka and the Videhas, and the Kosalas also, because their names have been woven into one of their national epics. The *Rámáyana* is as popular and as widely read by millions of Hindus to the present day as is the Mahábhárata; and thus the memory of the ancient civilization which the early Hindus developed in the Gangetic states is still cherished in the recollections of their modern descendants. It is difficult to say which portions of the story of the Rámáyana are based on facts, but as it reflects the manners and customs of the time, it should be told, however briefly, in a historical work.

Dasaratha, king of the Kosalas, had three queens honoured above others, of whom Kausalyá bore him his eldest son, Ráma; Kaikeyí was the mother of Bharata, and Sumitrá gave birth to Lakshmana and Satrughna. The young princes, according to the customs of the times, were versed in arms and also in the learning of the age, and Ráma, the eldest born, was as pious and truthful as he was distinguished in feats of arms. Dasaratha in his old age had decided on making Ráma the Yuvaraja or reigning prince; but the beauteous Kaikeyí insisted that her son should be Yuvaraja, and the feeble old king yielded to the determined will of his wife.

Before this, Ráma had won the daughter of Janaka,

king of the Videhas, at a great assembly. Kings and warriors had gathered there to wield a heavy bow, which was the feat required to win the princess's hand, but Ráma alone could lift it, and he bent it till it broke in twain. And now, when the town of Ayodhyá was ringing at the prospect of the installation of Ráma and his newly married consort, it was decided in Kaikeyí's chambers that her son Bharata must be Yuvaraja, and further that Ráma must go into exile for fourteen years.

The duteous Ráma submitted to his father's wishes. His faithful half-brother, Lakshmana, accompanied him, and the gentle Sítá would not part from her lord. Amidst the tears and lamentations of the people of Ayodhyá, Ráma and Sítá and Lakshmana departed from the city.

The old King Dasaratha did not long survive the banishment of his brave and beloved boy. A pathetic story is told that in his youth he had once gone out to hunt, and had accidentally shot a boy, and thus caused the death of an old and broken-hearted father. The curse of the deceased now had effect on Dasaratha with terrible severity, and the king of the Kosalas died in sorrow for his banished son.

Bharata now came to Ráma in the wilderness, and implored him to return to Ayodhyá as king. But the truthful Ráma felt that the promise he had made to his father was not dissolved by his death, and he proceeded on his journey in the wilderness, directing Bharata to return and reign as king.

For thirteen years the banished prince wandered with his wife and his devoted brother in Dándaka forest and towards the sources of the Godavari river. The whole of Southern India was then inhabited by non-Aryan aborigines. The poet has introduced them as monkeys and bears, and the non-Aryans of Ceylon are described as monsters.

Rávana, the monster-king of Ceylon, heard of the beauty of Sítá, now dwelling in the wilderness, and in the absence of Ráma took her away from their hut and carried her off to Ceylon. Ráma obtained a clue of her after long search; he made alliances with the barbarian tribes of Southern India, and prepared to cross over to Ceylon and win back his wife.

A natural causeway runs nearly across the strait between India and Ceylon. The poet imagines that this causeway was constructed by Ráma's army with huge boulders and rocks carried from the continent.

The army crossed over, and the town of Lánka was besieged. Chief after chief was sent out by Rávana to break through the besiegers and disperse their forces, but they all fell in the war. At last Rávana himself came out, and was killed by Ráma. Sítá was recovered, and she proved her untainted virtue by throwing herself into a lighted pyre and coming out uninjured.

The fourteenth year of exile being now passed, Ráma and Sítá returned to Ayodhyá and ascended the throne; but the suspicions of the people fell on Sítá, who could not, they thought, have returned untainted, and Ráma bowed to the suspicions of the people and sent poor suffering Sítá, with her unborn offspring, into exile.

Valmíki, a saint, and the reputed author of this epic, received her in his hermitage, and there her twin sons, Lava and Kusa, were born. Years passed by, the twins became manly and warlike boys, proficient in arms, and Valmíki composed the poem of the Rámáyana, and taught the boys to repeat it.

Then Ráma decided to celebrate the famous horse-sacrifice, as a token of his supreme sovereignty. A horse was sent out whom none might restrain without incurring the hostility of the great king of Ayodhyá. The animal came as far as Valmíki's hermitage, and the spirited and playful boys caught it and detained it. Ráma's guards in vain tried to recover the animal from the youthful warriors. At last Ráma himself came and saw the princely boys, but did not know who they were. He heard his own deeds chanted by them, and it was in a passion of grief and repentance that he at last knew them and embraced them as his own sons.

But there was no joy in store for Sítá. The people's suspicions could not be removed, and the earth, which had given poor Sítá birth, yawned and received its long-suffering child. Sítá in the Rig Veda is the field-furrow, worshipped as an agricultural deity; and the reader will see how this first conception of Sítá still asserts itself in the Rámáyana, in which she is described as born of the earth, and received back into the earth. But this allegory is lost to the Hindus of the present times; to them she is an all-suffering, devoted, saint-like wife. To this day Hindus hesitate to call their children by the name of Sítá; for if her gentleness, her virtue, her uncomplaining faith, and her unconquerable love to her lord were more than human, her sufferings and sorrows too were more than what usually fall to the lot of woman. There is not a Hindu woman in the length and breadth of India to whom the story of suffering Sítá is not known, and to whom her character is not a model and a pattern; and Ráma too is a model to men for his faithfulness, his obedience, and his piety. The Mahábhárata is a heroic epic, the Rámáyana is a didactic epic; and these two grand poems have been for the millions of India a means of moral education, the efficacy of which is not inferior to that of the Bible among Christian nations.

CHAPTER III.

MANNERS AND CIVILIZATION.

WE have in the last two chapters described the state of the Hindu nations of the Gangetic valley, their flourishing and prosperous kingdoms, their schools of learning, their elaborate religious rites and observances, and their settled and civilized life, contrasting with the ruder and less settled life of their ancestors of the Punjab. The wars with the aborigines were at an end; no foreign nations invaded India or influenced Hindu manners, no extraneous influences disturbed the even development of Hindu civilization. The great confederation of Hindu races, from the banks of the Jumna to those of the Gandak, lived by themselves; the outside world did not exist for them. The lofty Himálayas divided them from the nations of the north. Impenetrable forests and the Vindhya mountains separated them from the south. To the east, Bengal was yet undiscovered, uncivilized, and marshy; and their own sturdy kinsmen of the Punjab kept out all foreign invaders from the west. Within these limits the Hindu races lived in the Epic Age in a state of complete isolation from the world, such as has perhaps never been paralleled in ancient or modern times. The Kurus and the Panchálas, the Kosalas and the Videhas, and the other Gangetic tribes, lived in a world of their own, ignorant of any civilized religion or rites but their own, ignorant of any civilized language or learning save their own, identifying Hindus with mankind, and Hindu manners with civilized social law. It will be easily imagined that under the influence of an isolation so absolute and complete, the manners, laws, and social rules of the Hindus acquired a rigidity and fixedness unexampled among other nations of the world, ancient and modern.

In the Vedic Age, the Hindus were constantly engaged in wars with the aborigines; and long after they were subdued, the distinction between the conquerors and the conquered endured. The Aryan Hindus never mixed socially with the despised Dasyus even after the latter had been subdued, and had adopted the settled and civilized life of the conquerors; and thus was generated the first social distinction between men dwelling side by side in villages and towns, and living by cultivation and the same arts of peace.

This distinction between Aryans and Dasyus naturally suggested and led to other distinctions among the Aryans themselves in the Epic Age. As religious rites became more elaborate in the Epic Age, and as great kings in the Gangetic states prided themselves on the performance of vast sacrifices with endless rites and observances, it is easy to understand that priests, who alone could undertake such rites, rose in the estimation of the people, until they were regarded as aloof from the people, as a distinct and separate community—as a *caste*. They devoted their lifetime to learning these rites; they alone were able to perform them in all their details; and the inference in the popular mind was that they alone were worthy of the holy task. And when hereditary priests were thus separated from the people by their fancied sanctity and real knowledge of elaborate ritual, it was considered scarcely correct, on their part, to form mésalliances with the people outside their holy rank. They still condescended to choose brides from among the people, but maidens of priestly houses never gave their hands to men outside their circle; and this custom gradually became fixed and rigid, until the priests formed a separate caste—the Brahmans of India.

Similar causes led to the rise of the royal caste. In the Vedic Age the greatest kings, like Sudás, were but renowned warriors and leaders of hosts, owned cultivated lands and herds of cattle like other people, and were of the people. In the Epic Age kings ruled over more extensive kingdoms, lived in august and pompous courts, and were looked up to with veneration by the thousands of submissive and peaceful men who formed the body of the people. As kings thus became more august and more addicted to the forms of royalty, as the people became more submissive and enervated and loyal, it was not considered correct for maidens of the royal and military classes to marry men from the ranks, although warriors might still choose brides from the people. And thus the warriors of the Epic Age formed themselves into a separate caste—the Kshatriyas of India.

The mass of the Aryan people still retained their ancient name of Visa or Vaisya, and formed a separate caste—the Vaisyas of India; while the conquered aborigines, although they had now adopted the civilized life and the language of their conquerors, were still kept at arm's-length, and formed the lowest caste—the Súdras of India.

Similar distinctions have from time to time crept in among other nations, but have nowhere acquired the inflexible rigidity of the caste system of India. In Europe, for instance, the priests, the barons, and the humble people formed in the Middle Ages widely distinct communities, answering to some extent to the Brahmans, the Kshatriyas, and the Vaisyas of antiquity. But the priests of mediæval Europe did not marry, and were recruited from the ablest and cleverest of the people. The knights, too, were glad to welcome into their ranks the bravest warriors from any grade of society. And the sturdy people themselves fought for their liberties and their chartered rights on battlefields and in council-halls, and gradually rose in power, in influence, and in wealth, until the marked distinctions of the Middle Ages were obliterated. The influences of modern civilization, which have united not only different classes of people, but distinct races and tribes into nations in Europe, have not been felt in India until within the last hundred years; and thus the ancient distinctions of caste, considerably modified and multiplied, still exist in modern India, a mystery and a marvel to all foreigners.

While the Aryan Hindus were thus divided into three separate castes in the Epic Age, they still enjoyed, however, the common privileges of Aryans, namely, the acquisition of religious learning and the practice of religious rites. We have elsewhere stated that Hindu boys left their parents at an early age, and lived with their Gurus or teachers for years to acquire a knowledge of the Vedas and the sciences as then known. Clever young men then went to Parishads and other seats of learning, and often a boy of one race, Kuru or Panchála, travelled to renowned schools of learning in the land of the Videhas or of the Kásís to acquire all that the age could teach. There was indeed a friendly rivalry among the cultured races of the Gangetic states in this respect; and even when they were at war with each other, their seats of learning, their religious hermitages, and their renowned sages and teachers were always respected. The descendants of the ancient Vasishthas and Viswámitras and Gautamas of the Vedic Age kept up the reputation of their families for learning and religious lore, and renowned sages of these families were invited to all royal courts, and rewarded by all cultured kings. Janaka of Videha yielded to none in his respect for learning, and an account which is preserved to us in the *Brihadáranyaka Upanishad* of a great assemblage at his court will illustrate the manners of the times.

"Janaka Videha performed a sacrifice at which many presents were offered to the priests. Brahmans of the Kurus and the Panchálas had come thither, and Janaka wished to know which of the Brahmans was the best read. So he enclosed a thousand cows, and ten *padas* of gold were fastened to each pair of horns.

"And Janaka spoke to them :

"'Ye venerable Brahmans, he who among ye is the wisest, let him drive away these cows.' Then those Brahmans durst not, but Yájnavalkya said to his pupil, 'Drive them away, my dear.' He replied, 'O glory of Sáman !' and drove them away."

The assembled Brahmans became angry at this presumption, and plied the proud Yájnavalkya with abstruse questions, but Yájnavalkya was a match for them all. There was one in that great assembly—and this is a remarkable fact, which illustrates the manners of the ancient Hindus—who was not deficient in the learning of the times although she was a lady. She rose in the open assembly and said :—

"O Yájnavalkya, as the son of a warrior from the Kásís or Videhas might string his loosened bow, take two pointed foe-piercing arrows in his hand, and rise to battle, I have risen to fight thee with two questions. Answer me these questions." The questions were put and answered, and the lady was silent, and the assembly acknowledged the superior learning of Yájnavalkya.

Passages like this throw much light on the manners of the ancient Hindus and the position of their women in society. There was as yet no unhealthy restraint on their movements, and they had a share in the learning of the times. They took a part in sacrifices and religious duties, they attended great assemblies, and they had their legitimate influence in society. Impartial students of ancient history will admit that women held a more honoured place among the ancient Hindus than among the ancient Greeks and Romans.

Young men, when they completed their education, were allowed to marry and to settle down as householders. Husband and wife then lighted the domestic sacrificial fire and offered daily oblations, and the fire was ever kept lighted in the houses of all pious Hindus. Besides daily oblations, numerous religious rites were prescribed, either at different seasons of the year, or at the time of certain domestic occurrences, and some account of these rites will be given in a subsequent chapter. It is enough to state here that while kings and wealthy men delighted in elaborate sacrifices, all pious Hindus, be they rich or poor, performed their little rites at their domestic firesides. No idol was worshipped, and no temple was known; the descendants of the Vedic Hindus still went through their religious ceremonies in their own homes, and offered oblations and prayers according to ancient rule.

Hospitality to strangers is prescribed as a religious obligation, while the essence of a Hindu's duties is inculcated in such passages as these :—

"Speak the truth. Do thy duty. Do not neglect the study of the Veda. After having brought to thy teacher the proper reward, marry and beget children. Do not swerve from truth. Do not swerve from duty. Do not neglect what is useful. Do not neglect greatness. Do not neglect the teaching of the Veda.

"Do not neglect the sacrifices due to the gods and the fathers. Let thy mother be to thee like unto a god. Let thy father be to thee like unto a god. Blameless acts should be regarded, not others. Good works performed by us should be regarded by thee."—*Taittirîyaka Upanishad.*

The wealth of rich men consisted in gold and silver and jewels, in cars, horses, cows, mules, and slaves, in houses and fertile lands, and herds of cattle. The use of gold and silver, of tin, lead, and iron was well known. Elephants had been domesticated, and we are often told of rich presents of elephants and cars and slave-girls with graceful ornaments on their necks. Rice, wheat, barley, and other kinds of grain were the food of the people, and various preparations of milk were relished. The flesh of the cow was an article of food, and some wine was consumed at sacrifices.

We have said before that Hindu women in these ancient times had their legitimate influence on society. Child-marriage, which is now practised in India, was unknown then, and the stories of the epics which we have narrated will show that royal princesses were married after they had attained womanhood. The marriage of widows, which is now prohibited among Hindus, was allowed in ancient times, and the rites which a widow had to perform before she entered into the married state again are distinctly laid down. Marriage among blood relations to the third or fourth generation was prohibited.

The study of the Vedas was considered the most important duty and the most cherished heritage of all Hindus. The Vedas were supposed to embody all the learning which it was given to man to acquire; and it is curious to note that as the infant sciences came into existence in India, they were considered as supplementary to the Vedas, and as helps to the performance of Vedic rites. Indeed, it is not an exaggeration to state that the sphere of knowledge was enlarged, and the sciences were discovered in India in the pursuit of religious rites and observances. A thoughtful writer and student of Hindu literature* rightly remarks: "The want of some rule by which to fix the right time for the sacrifices gave the first impulse to astronomical observations; urged by this want, the priest remained watching night after night the advance of the moon through the circle of the *Nakshatras*, and day after day the alternate progress of the sun towards the north and the south. The laws of phonetics were investigated because the wrath of the gods followed the wrong pronunciation of a single letter of the sacrificial formulas; grammar and etymology had the task of securing the right understanding of the holy texts. The connection of philosophy and theology—so close that it was impossible to decide where the one ends and the other begins—is too well known to require any comment."

These were the sciences which were cultivated in the schools of learning of the Gangetic states; and it is an important fact in the history of the Hindus that all these sciences sprang from the practice of their religious rites. The writer whom we have quoted above lays down the principle which all Indian historians recognize, that whatever science "is closely connected with ancient Indian religion must be considered as having sprung up among the Indians themselves."

An elementary knowledge of astronomy was acquired by the Hindus in the Vedic Age, but it was in the Epic Age that this science received much development. The year was divided into twelve lunar months, and a thirteenth month was added every fifth year to adjust the lunar year with the solar year. The twenty-eight *Nakshatras* or constellations through which the moon passed in her monthly journey were observed and named. The progress of the sun to the north and to the south of the

* Dr. Thibaut.

equator was noted, and the position of the solstitial points was also marked. An observation of the position of the solstitial points was made when the compilation of the Vedas was completed, and some mathematicians have calculated from this that the event took place in 1181 B.C.

The study of other sciences was prosecuted in the Epic Age. Grammar, etymology, phonetics, and prosody were cultivated with great care, as they regulated the proper utterance of prayers, as the position of the heavenly bodies fixed the auspicious moments for sacrifices. Attention was also paid to ethics and ratiocination. Arithmetic is pre-eminently a Hindu science, and was developed as early as the Epic Age, while minute rules for the construction of altars of different shapes and sizes, led to the discovery of geometrical principles, as we shall see in the next Book.

The administration of law was still rude, and, as among other ancient nations, trial by the ordeal of fire was recognized. To discover the truth was the end and object of law, and law was described as truth. "If a man declares what is true, they say he declares the law; and if he declares the law, they say he declares what is true. Both are the same."—*Brihadáranyaka Upanishad.*

CHAPTER IV.

RELIGION.

THE gradual change which crept over the spirit of the religion of the Hindus in the Epic Age has already been indicated. The increase in wealth and civilization, and the comparatively settled and easy life of the people, gave birth to a taste for great and pompous sacrifices; and a hereditary priestly caste naturally attached great importance to the forms and ceremonials which accompanied these rites. And in the performance of these elaborate sacrifices the attention of the worshipper was to a great extent diverted from the deities, who were the true objects of devotion, to the minutiæ of rites, the erection of altars, the fixing of the proper astronomical moments for lighting the fire, the correct pronunciation of prayers, and to the various requisite acts accompanying a sacrifice.

The literature of a nation is but the reflection of the national mind; and when the nation turned its religion into forms and ceremonials, religious literature became to some extent inane and lifeless. We miss in the voluminous Brahmanas of this age the fervency and earnestness of the Vedic hymns. We find, on the other hand, grotesque reasons given for every minute rite, dogmatic explanations of texts, penances for every breach of form and rule, and elaborate directions for every act and movement of the worshipper. The works show a degree of credulity and submission on the part of the people, and of absolute power on the part of the priests, which remind us of the Middle Ages in Europe.

We willingly leave this subject and turn to the legends contained in the Bráhmanas, some of which are interesting. That which is the best known in Europe is one resembling the account of the deluge in the Old Testament. Manu, the mythical progenitor of man, was washing his hands when a fish came unto him and said, "Rear me; I will save thee". Manu reared the fish, and it told him, "In such and such a year the flood will come Thou shalt then attend to me by preparing a ship." The flood came, and Manu entered into the ship, which he had built in time, and the fish swam up to him and carried the ship beyond the northern mountain. The ship was fastened to a tree, and when the flood subsided Manu descended. "The flood swept away all the creatures, and Manu alone remained here."—*Satapatha Bráhmana.*

In some of the legends of the Bráhmanas we notice how poetical similes used in the Rig Veda were transformed into mythological tales. The simile of the sun pursuing the Dawn-goddess lent itself easily to a tale of Prajápati seducing his daughter, and thus creating and peopling this universe. Hindu commentators saw the origin of this myth, and the learned Kumárila, who lived some five centuries after Christ, thus explains it :—

"Prajápati, the Lord of Creation, is the name of the sun, and he is called so because he protects all creatures. His daughter Ushas is the dawn; and when it is said that he was in love with her, this only means that at sunrise the sun runs after the dawn."

Various other accounts of the creation are given in the different Bráhmanas. We are told in the *Taittiríyaka Bráhmana* that in the beginning nothing was except water, and a lotus leaf stood out of it. Prajápati dived in the shape of a boar and brought up some earth, and spread it out, and fastened it down by pebbles. That was the earth.

In the *Satapatha Bráhmana* we are told that the gods and the Asuras (enemies of gods) both sprang from Prajápati, and the earth trembled like a lotus leaf when the gods and Asuras contended for mastery. And elsewhere in the same Bráhmana we are told, "Verily in the beginning Prajápati existed alone." He created living beings, and birds and reptiles and snakes, but they all passed away for want of food. He then made the breasts (of mammals) teem with milk, and so the living creatures survived.

These examples will suffice. We have seen that the Hindus of the Vedic Age were led from the worship of Nature up to Nature's God, and were able to conceive the great idea that in the beginning nothing existed except the Deity, and that the whole universe was his handiwork. The more speculative Hindus of the Epic Age reproduced the same idea, and their various guesses as to the way in which God created the universe are among the earliest conjectures of man into the mysteries of creation. But nobler and more earnest efforts were made in this Epic Age to know the unknown God, and these strivings of the Hindu mind are imbedded in the works called the *Upanishads*, of which we have spoken before, and which are among the most remarkable works in the literature of the world.

The idea of a Universal Soul, of an All-pervading Breath, is the keystone of the philosophy and thought of the Upanishads. This idea is somewhat different from monotheism, as it has been generally understood by other nations. The monotheism of other nations recognizes a God and Creator as distinct from the created beings, but the monotheism of the Upanishads, which has been the monotheism of the Hindus ever since, recognizes God as the Universal Being;—all things have emanated from him, are a part of him, and will resolve themselves into him.

This is the truth which the poor fatherless boy Satyakáma learnt from the great book of Nature. He was a poor child of a poor servant-girl, and did not know who his father was. When he came to a Guru to learn according to the custom of the times, and the Guru asked after his family, the truthful boy replied, "I do not know, sir, of what family I am. I asked my mother, and she answered, 'In my youth, when I had to move about much as a servant, I conceived thee. I do not know of what family thou art.'" The Guru was pleased with the truth-loving boy, and kept him in his house.

And the boy, according to the custom of the times, served his teacher menially, and went out to tend his cattle; and in course of time he learnt the great truth which Nature, and even the brute creation, teach those whose minds are open to instruction. He learnt the truth from the herd which he tended, from the fire that he lighted, from the flamingo and diver-bird that flew around him when in the evening he had penned his cows and laid wood on the evening-fire. His teacher was struck, and asked, "Friend, you shine like one who knows God; who then has taught you?" "Not men," was the young student's reply. And the truth which he had learnt was that the four quarters, and the earth, the sky, the heavens beyond, and the ocean, and the sun, the moon, the lightning and the fire, and the organs and minds of living beings—yea, the whole universe, was God.—*Chhándogya Upanishad.*

This is the truth which the learned priest Yájnavalkya explained to his beloved wife Maitreyí when she refused all wealth which her husband offered to her, and thirsted for that which would make her immortal; and the priest, gratified by the noble wish of his spouse, then explained to her that the Universal Soul dwells in the husband and in the wife and in the sons, in Brahmans and in Kshatriyas, and in all living beings, in the gods above and in the creatures below—yea, in all the universe.—*Brihadáranyaka Upanishad.*

This is the truth which is inculcated in numerous passages in the Upanishads in language simple and fervent and solemn, the like of which has never been composed by Hindus of later times.

"The Intelligent, whose body is spirit, whose form is bright, whose thoughts are true, whose nature is like ether (omnipresent and invisible), from whom all works, all desires, all sweet odours and tastes proceed;—He who embraces all this, who never speaks and is never surprised,

"He is my soul within the heart, smaller than a corn of rice, smaller than a corn of barley, smaller than a mustard-seed or kernel of a canary-seed. He also is my soul within my heart, greater than the earth, greater than the sky, greater than the heavens beyond, greater than all these worlds.

"He from whom all works, all desires, all sweet odours and tastes proceed, who embraces all this, who never speaks and is never surprised, He—my soul within my heart—is God. When I shall have departed from hence, I shall mingle with him."—*Chhándogya Upanishad.*

This is the truth which is explained in a hundred beautiful similes. The Universal Soul is like the honey, in which drops collected by bees from distant trees mingle; it is like the ocean, in which rivers coming from distant regions are lost; it is like the saline water, in which particles of salt can no longer be discerned.

"At whose wish does the mind, sent forth, proceed on

its errand?" asks the pupil. "At whose command does the first breath go forth? At whose wish do we utter this speech? What god directs the eye or the ear?"

The teacher replies: "It is the ear of the ear, the mind of the mind, the speech of the speech, the breath of the breath, the eye of the eye. . . . That which is not expressed by speech, but by which speech is expressed, . . . that which does not think by mind, but by which mind is thought, . . . that which does not see by the eye, but by which one sees, . . . that which does not hear by the ear, but which by the hearing is heard, . . . that which does not breathe by breath, but by which breath is breathed, —that alone is God—not that which people here adore." —*Kena Upanishad.*

It is easy to see in the above passage an effort made by the sages and thinking men in the ancient age to shake themselves from the trammels of meaningless ceremonials and the fanciful gods whom "people here adore," and to soar to a higher region of thought, to comprehend the incomprehensible, the breath of the breath and the mind of the mind. It was a manly and fervent effort made by the Hindus three thousand years ago to know the unknown God; and the daring but pious thinkers thus describe the Deity whom they tried to conceive:—

"He, the Soul, encircled all bright, incorporeal, scatheless, without muscles, pure, untouched by evil, a seer, wise, omnipresent and self-existent,—He disposed all things rightly for eternal years."—*I'sá Upanishad.*

Such were the earliest efforts made by the Hindus to discern the attributes and nature of the unknown Deity. They are among the earliest efforts of man to comprehend his maker, and we find them in the imperishable works of the Hindus, the Upanishads.

Another new and startling idea is also first met with in these works. Other nations have believed in the resurrection of the soul; the Hindus believed in the past as well as in the future existence of the soul; and this idea of the transmigration of souls is first taught and explained in the Upanishads.

The idea is that the same soul passes through various bodies according to its acts, before it can be freed from all its imperfections and mingle in the Deity. "According to his deeds and according to his knowledge, he is born again as a worm, or as an insect, or as a fish, or as a bird, or as a lion, or as a boar, or as a serpent, or as a tiger, or as a man, or as something else in different places." And after passing through various worlds, the purified soul approaches God.—*Kaushitaki Upanishad.*

This doctrine of transmigration of souls, which was first taught in India, and which other ancient nations borrowed from the Hindus, is explained in many beautiful similes. The progress of the soul through different bodies is like the progress of the caterpillar moving from blade to blade, or like the changes in the gold which the goldsmith turns into newer and more beautiful forms. And when at last the soul is thus purified of all its imperfections, it finally casts off the body and mingles with God. "As the slough of the snake lies on an anthill, dead and cast away, thus lies the body; but the disembodied immortal spirit is God, it is Light."—*Brihadáranyaka Upanishad.*

The creation of the world also puzzled the sages of the Upanishads. We are told in the *Chhándogya* that the Self-existent grew into an egg, and the egg burst itself into two halves, the heaven and the earth. And elsewhere in the same work we are told that the Self-existent first sent forth fire, and the fire sent forth water, and the water sent forth the earth.

The *Aitareya A'ranyaka* discusses the first material

from which the universe was created; and, as in the Rig Veda and in the Jewish account of the creation, water is said to be the first material cause.

And in the *Brihadáranyaka Upanishad* we are told that the self-existent Soul formed himself into the male and the female, and the creation proceeded therefrom.

The mysteries of death were no less strange to the early sages than the mysteries of creation, and a beautiful legend is told of a sage, Nachiketas, who asked Death to reveal his mysteries. But Death was unwilling to reveal his secrets, and said—

"Choose sons and grandsons who shall live a hundred years, herds of cattle, elephants, horses, gold. Choose the wide abode of the earth, and live thyself as many harvests as thou desirest.

"If you can think of any boon equal to that, choose wealth and long life. Be king, Nachiketas, on the whole earth. I make thee the enjoyer of all desires.

"Whatever desires are difficult to attain among mortals, ask for them, anything to thy wish. These fair maidens with chariots and musical instruments, such are indeed not to be obtained by men,—be waited on by them whom I give thee, but do not ask me about dying."

But Nachiketas said, "These things last till to-morrow, O Death! for they wear out the vigour of all the senses. Even the whole of life is short. Keep thou thy horses, keep dance and song for thyself."

Pressed by the pious inquirer, Death at last revealed his great secret, which is the cardinal idea of Hindu monotheism.

"The wise who by meditation of his own soul recognizes the soul . . . as God,—he indeed leaves joy and sorrow far behind.

"A mortal who has heard this and accepted this,—who has separated it from all qualities, and has reached the subtle Being,—rejoices because he has cause for rejoicing. The house of God is open, I believe, O Nachiketas."—*Katha Upanishad.*

Such were the efforts of the Hindus of the Epic Age to learn the mysteries of the Deity and of the soul, of creation and of death. And though in these ancient ideas we find much that is fanciful, and though they are clothed in quaint similes and legends, yet it is impossible not to be struck with the freshness, the earnestness, and the vigour of thought which mark these yearnings after the truth. A great German philosopher, Schopenhauer, has recorded his high admiration for the Upanishads in striking words which have been often quoted. "From every sentence, deep, original, and sublime thoughts arise, and the whole is pervaded by a high and holy and earnest spirit. Indian air surrounds us and original thoughts of kindred spirits. . . . It has been the solace of my life ; it will be the solace of my death."

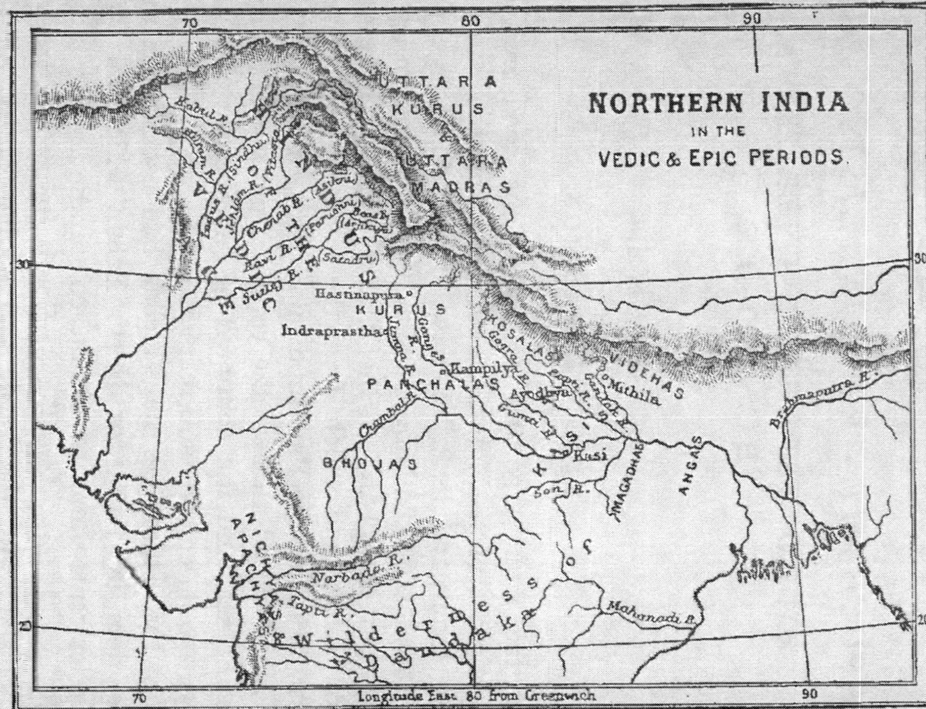
NORTHERN INDIA
IN THE
VEDIC & EPIC PERIODS
UTTARA KURUS
UTTARA MADRAS
Kabul R.
Indus R.
Jhelum R.
Chenab R.
Ravi R.
Sutlej R.
Hastinapura
KURUS
Indraprastha
Jumna R.
Ganges R.
Kampilya
PANCHALAS
Chambal R.
BHOJAS
KOSALAS
Gogra R.
Ayodhya
Gumti R.
VIDEHAS
Mithila
Gandak R.
KASIS
Kasi
Son R.
MAGADHAS
ANGAS
Brahmaputra R.
Narbada R.
Tapti R.
Mahanadi R.
Longitude East 80 from Greenwich
70
80
90
30
20
E.S Weller.

EPOCH III.—RATIONALISTIC AGE.

HINDU EXPANSION OVER INDIA. B.C. 1000–320.

CHAPTER I.

HINDU EXPANSION.

In the Vedic Age the Hindu Aryans conquered the aborigines of the Punjab, and settled on the banks of the Indus and its tributaries. In the Epic Age they founded powerful kingdoms in the Gangetic valley as far down as Behar. In the third age, of which we shall now speak, and which, from the tenor of its literature, may be called the Philosophical or Rationalistic Age, the Hindus spread all over the country from the Himálayas to the sea, and the continent of India received Hindu civilization, culture, and religion.

In the Epic Age the Videhas had established their kingdom in Tirhút or North Behar, which was then the extreme limit of Hindu colonization; but it was not long before Magadha or South Behar was likewise colonized; and the hardy and warlike natives of that province rapidly rose in power after they had received extraneous culture, so that, in course of time, Magadha became the most powerful kingdom in India.

When the war of the Mahábhárata was fought, probably in the thirteenth century before Christ, Magadha is said to have been ruled by a rude and sturdy warrior, Jarásandha. A list of twenty-eight kings who ruled after Jarásandha is preserved in Hindu records, but the authenticity of the list is doubtful, and nothing is known of the kings except their names.

It was about 600 B.C. that Sisunága began a new dynasty, which is known after his name, and gave to Magadha the first place among the Hindu kingdoms of India. Fourth in descent from Sisunága was the wise and beneficent king Bimbisára, who reigned over fifty years, from 537 to 485 B.C. His rule will ever remain memorable in the history of India and of the world, because the great religious teacher, Gautama Buddha, of the Sákya race, preached in his reign that noble religion which is now followed by a third of the human race.

Bimbisára is said to have been killed by his son Ajátasatru, who ruled for over thirty years, from 485 to 453 B.C., and largely extended the limits of the kingdom. Anga, or East Behar, was then under the rule of Magadha, and Ajátasatru widened his boundaries to the west and north by subduing the Kosalas and other ancient races. A race of Turanians called Vajji had also poured through the Himalayas and settled in North Behar. Ajátasatru built the town of Pátaliputra, or Patna, to keep them back.

Four princes of the Sisunága dynasty ruled after Ajátasatru, and the dynasty came to a close about 370 B.C.

Nanda and his eight sons then reigned for about fifty years. It was in the reign of the last prince of the Nanda dynasty that Alexander the Great invaded the Punjab. Chandragupta, a rebel whom Nanda had exiled, joined Alexander, and lived for some time in his camp; but he had ultimately to fly for his life when Alexander became disgusted with his pride and haughtiness. After the departure of Alexander, Chandragupta gathered around him the hardy warriors of the Punjab, conquered Magadha, and founded a new dynasty about 320 B.C. For the first time he united the whole of Northern India under one rule, and a new epoch of Indian history begins, therefore, with this great emperor. The Rationalistic Epoch ends at this date, *i.e.*, about the time of Alexander's death.

It may be easily imagined that while Magadha enjoyed such power and civilization for centuries, the surrounding kingdoms were not left in the dark. Anga was directly under the rule of Magadha; while Vanga or East Bengal, and Kalinga or South Bengal, received the first rays of Hindu civilization in this age. By the close of the fourth century, these places had become the seats of powerful Hindu kingdoms.

Gujrat was early colonized by the Hindus, and it would appear from the legends of Krishna in the Mahábhárata that the country was colonized from the banks of the Jumna by some of the races who had fought in the great war; and by the fourth century before Christ the Suráshtras of Gujrat had become a powerful nation. Malwa, too, was early Hinduized, and the kings of Ujain were reckoned among the civilized Hindu powers in the Rationalistic Age.

The waves of Hindu conquest and colonization rolled farther, and the Vindhya mountains were crossed. A great and powerful kingdom, that of the Andhras, was founded in the country between the Narbada and the Kistna rivers, and the capital of this southern empire was situated near modern Amarávatí. So well did the Andhras adopt the civilization of the Hindus, that they established schools of Hindu learning within their country; and the name of A'pastamba, who was born in the Dekhan in this age, is as renowned as that of Gautama or Vasishtha of Northern India.

Still farther rolled the waves of Aryan influence, and the country beyond the Kistna river received Aryan civilization and religion. Three kingdoms, those of the Cholas, the Cheras, and the Pandyas, had arisen in the extreme southern part of India several centuries before the Christian era, and they existed side by side for many centuries. Pandya, which was to the extreme south, is said to have been first visited from the north by Aryan Hindus who came from Gujrat by sea.

And lastly, the island of Ceylon was visited by Hindu merchants for its ivory and pearls, and thus became known to them. In the fifth century before Christ, Vijaya, the son of Sinhavâhu, a king of Magadha, is said to have been exiled by his father for acts of fraud and violence, and to have come by sea, conquered the island, and founded a Hindu kingdom there.

Thus by the fourth century before Christ, the whole of India, except deserts and wild tracts, was the seat of powerful Hindu kingdoms, or of kingdoms that had received Hindu culture and Hindu religion.

We have said before that Chandragupta ascended the throne of Magadha about 320 B.C. An intelligent Greek observer, Megasthenes, the ambassador of the Greek king Seleucus of Bactria, lived in Chandragupta's capital for five years, from 317 to 312 B.C., and the testimony of the observant Greek bears out what we know from Hindu records of the expansion of the Hindus all over India before the fourth century. Megasthenes found the Magadhas as rulers of Northern India from the Punjab to Behar; and Chandragupta, the king of the Magadhas, had a standing army of 600,000 foot-soldiers, 30,000 horse, and 9000 elephants, "whence may be formed some conjecture," says the Greek, "as to the vastness of his resources". To the east, Bengal and Orissa were parcelled into separate kingdoms, and the king of Kalinga had 60,000 foot-soldiers, 1000 horse, and 700 elephants. To the south, the Andhras had thirty walled towns within their vast dominions, and 100,000 infantry, 2000 cavalry, and 1000 elephants. To the west, the Saurashtras of Gujrat were a powerful race, with 150,000 infantry, 5000 horse, and 1600 elephants, and their capital on the sea-coast was a great emporium of maritime trade. And even Ceylon was known to Megasthenes, and was famous for its gold, its pearl-fisheries, and its large breed of elephants.

If, now, we compare the state of the Hindu world, confined to the valleys of the Indus and the Ganges in the eleventh century before Christ, with the state of the Hindu world, embracing the whole of India in the fourth century before Christ, we comprehend the political history of the seven centuries which constitute the Rationalistic Age.

Nothing strikes us more forcibly than the enterprise and vigour of the Hindu colonists and conquerors; for India was still a vast and unknown continent at the commencement of the Rationalistic Age. Out of over a million square miles of habitable land in India, not much more than a hundred thousand square miles were explored and colonized in the Vedic and Epic Ages. The sturdy warriors who fought for centuries against the aborigines of the Punjab, and their enterprising descendants, who poured down the valley of the Ganges and ruled in flourishing and civilized kingdoms for centuries more, had effected much in their day; but they had as yet touched only the fringe of the great continent. No doubt they had settled in the best portions of that continent, in the fertile valleys of the Indus and the Ganges; but the whole of India lay beyond, unknown and unexplored, and filled by strange tribes who knew not of Aryan culture or Aryan religion.

And when poets of the Epic Age tried to describe these unknown tribes, they could only draw on their imagination, and picture them as monkeys, bears, monsters.

It was the Hindus of the third age who at last conquered, or at least came in actual contact with them, civilized them, made them Hindus, and included their countries within the pale of the Hindu world. The task of mere conquest is easy enough, and in more recent times vast hordes of barbarians like the Huns and the Moguls have swept across the old world, almost from ocean to ocean. But the Hindus of the Rationalistic Age were less a conquering than a civilizing race. Whereever they conquered they introduced cultivation, manufactures, and the arts of peace. Wherever they went, they spread the Sanscrit language, the Vedic rites, the Hindu religion. Wherever they settled, they founded Hindu schools of law, religion, and learning. Wherever they colonized, they Hinduized the population and founded Hindu kingdoms. Bengal and Orissa were Hindu king doms in the fourth century B.C. Suráshtra was a powerful Hindu maritime country; the Andhras founded renowned Hindu schools of learning; and even the Pandyas, the Cheras and the Cholas, cultivated Hindu learning in Kanchi and other classical towns of their own, and formed a portion of the vast confederation of Hindu nations. This is the distinctive feature of the work of the Rationalistic Age; the whole of India was not merely conquered and reduced to military subjection, it received the mantle of Hindu religion and civilization.

The earlier Hindus of the Punjab and the Gangetic valley had almost exterminated or expelled the aborigines of those regions, and to the present day the Hindus of Northern India are almost pure Aryans. But the work of extermination or expulsion could not proceed over a whole continent like India; and in the Rationalistic

Age, therefore, the Hindu colonists civilized and Hinduized the aboriginal races without expelling them. The mass of the population of Bengal and Southern India therefore remain to this day,—what they were in the Rationalistic Age,—Hindus by religion, language, and civilization, but mostly non-Aryans by descent.

The fishing and hunting tribes of marshy Bengal, like the Kaibartas and Chandálas, rapidly learnt Hindu arts, Hindu language, and Hindu religion; and dwelt peacefully under the Aryan emigrants, whose descendants form the higher castes of Bengal to this day. In the south, the number of Hindu immigrants was still less, and the aboriginal tribes, in adopting the Hindu religion, selected priests and Brahmans of their own races. The purity of Aryan descent is lost more and more as we travel farther from the Gangetic valley.

Hindu writers noticed this distinction and expressed it in their own way. The fact is so curious that we will illustrate it by quoting a passage from Baudháyana, who probably flourished six centuries before Christ.

"Some declare the country between the Jumna and the Ganges to be the *A'rya-land*. . . .

"The inhabitants of Avanti (Malwa), of Anga (East Behar), of Magadha (South Behar), of Suráshtra (Gujrat), of the Dekhan, of Upávrit, of Sindh, and the Sauvírás (South Punjab) *are of mixed origin.*

"He who has visited the A'rattas (of the Punjab), the Káraskaras (of Southern India), the Pundras (of North Bengal), the Sauvíras (of South Punjab), the Vangas (of East Bengal), the Kalingas (of South Bengal and Orissa), or the Pránúnas, *shall offer a sacrifice.*"

It is most remarkable how this ancient writer divides India into three distinct belts, which were regarded with different degrees of esteem, because the purity of Aryan descent differed in these regions. The pure Aryan population of the Gangetic valley were regarded with the highest esteem. South Behar and East Behar, South Punjab, Sindh, and Gujrat, Malwa and the Dekhan formed the second belt, because they had been colonized by Aryan Hindus early in the Rationalistic Age, and contained a fair mixture of pure Aryans. Bengal and Orissa and Southern India had scarcely yet been Hinduized at that time, and contained little Aryan blood; thus these countries were considered so unholy that people who travelled there had to perform a penance.

Thus, then, the Magadhas, the Angas, the Bengalis, the Suráshtras, the Andhras of the Dekhan, and the tribes south of the Kistna river, were ancient non-Aryan nations, who received Hindu religion and civilization from Hindu Aryans who conquered them or settled in their countries, mixed with them, and taught them all that a cultured nation can teach less civilized neighbours. The Sanscrit hymns, which were composed on the banks of the Sarasvati and chanted in Hastinápura and Mithilá, were now uttered in Amarávatí and Kánchí; the Vedic rites which were performed on the Jumna and the Sarayu were now performed on the Godavari and the Kistna; and the mantle of Hindu civilization and Hindu religion fell on new nations now included within the pale of Hinduism. All India became the Hindu world, and the numerous subjugated races of India studied the Hindu language, practised Hindu rites, and bore the livery of Hinduism.

It is not, therefore, a fanciful analogy to compare the Hindu world before the time of Alexander with the Greek world after Alexander's death. Greece itself, like the Gangetic valley, was the original home of the culture and religion which spread far and wide. The Macedonians, like the Magadhas, learnt that culture from the nation they conquered; and remoter nations, both in the Hindu world and in the Greek world, received the same light.

Greek religion was proclaimed, Greek sculpture was imitated, Greek philosophy was studied, and the Greek language was spoken and written in Italy and in Sicily, in Egypt and in Syria, in Persia and in Bactria. The genius of Greece was like a torchlight for remote nations, and Italy, Egypt, and Western Asia proudly wore the livery of Greek civilization, as the nations of India wore the livery of Hindu culture and religion.

Nor does the historical parallel end here. The civilization of the Greeks has been effaced from Asia and Africa, but it has endured and fructified among the nations of Europe, as the civilization of the Gangetic Hindus has fructified among the nations of India for over two thousand years; and the sacred tongue which was spoken in Kámpilya and Ayodhyá is still cultivated with as much regard in Bombay and Bengal as the Greek language is studied in the learned universities of Oxford, Paris, and Berlin.

CHAPTER II.

MANNERS AND CIVILIZATION.

As the Hindu colonists spread over the whole of India, and imposed on other nations the customs and rites of Aryan Hindus, it became necessary to compile condensed manuals or codes of such rites and laws. Learning was yet imparted by rote, and the nations of Hinduized India developed a form of composition in which teachers could teach and learners could learn by rote. Indeed, the writers of the period went from one extreme to another, and the verbose *Bráhmana* literature of the Epic Age was now replaced by *Sútras* or aphorisms in the Rationalistic Age. So condensed and brief is this form of composition, that it is often difficult to gather the sense without the help of commentaries; and so much trouble was taken by the writers of the period to abbreviate and condense their sentences, that the saying became proverbial that "An author rejoiceth in the economising of half a short vowel as much as in the birth of a son".

Details of ceremonials relating to Vedic sacrifices were compressed into practical condensed manuals which were called *Srauta Sútras*. Rules of petty homely rites or appropriate season festivals were similarly condensed into manuals called *Grihya Sútras*. And lastly, the civil and criminal and social laws of the Hindus were compiled into *Dharma Sútras*. These three descriptions of Sútras throw much light on the manners and customs of the age.

The Vedic rites prescribed by the Srauta Sútras are numerous; but they have been classified by Gautama, a writer of the period, into fourteen principal forms of sacrifice. It is needless to detail them here, but one or two have already been alluded to in previous chapters. Thus when the student completed his studies, and married and settled down as a householder, his first duty was to light the sacrificial fire, and this ancient rite was called *Agniádhána.* The fire was lighted generally by friction, and the newly married couple performed various ceremonies and remained awake the whole night and kept up the fire. And pious Hindu householders kept up this sacrificial fire all through their lives, and offered oblations to it when sacrificing. A simple oblation of milk offered morning and evening to this fire was called the *Agnihotra* rite, and was the simplest of the Vedic rites.

The petty homely rites prescribed by the Grihya Sútras were also numerous, but have been classified by Gautama into seven principal forms. The most important of these is the *Sráddha,* or oblations offered periodically to deceased ancestors. The sacrificer offered the Arghya water with appropriate words, as "Father, this is thy Arghya; grandfather, this is thy Arghya; great-grandfather, this is thy Arghya." Brahmans endowed with learning, moral character, and correct conduct were invited and fed as representatives of departed ancestors, and gifts of perfumes, garlands, incense, lights and clothes were made to them. The remaining Grihya rites are of smaller importance, and are generally season festivals. There were rites for the full moon and new moon nights, a rite for the rainy season to propitiate the snakes, a rite when the autumn harvest was reaped, and another more favourite rite when the great winter harvest was gathered in, and various sweetmeats and cakes were prepared and distributed by skilful Hindu matrons and maids.

Besides these seven Grihya rites, there were other ceremonies of a purely domestic character, in which the ancient Hindu rejoiced on every appropriate occasion. Gautama classifies them under nineteen heads, and some of them are interesting. Three distinct ceremonies at different periods were performed by the rejoicing husband when his wife gave promise of an heir, and three more were performed on the birth of a child or when it first took solid food. As years passed on and the boy became fit to commence his studies, the rite of tonsure was followed by the rite of initiation, by which last ceremony the young student was handed over to his Guru or teacher, to live with him for years, and to learn the sacred knowledge which it was the duty of all Hindus to acquire. Four different ceremonies were performed when the sacred Veda was studied; and when the young student at last completed his education, he went through the ceremonial of a bath, and then through the marriage rite, and entered into the status of a householder. The more onerous duties of a householder commenced from this period, and five daily rites were prescribed for him, consisting of offerings to gods and departed fathers, to men and to spirits, and lastly to the Supreme Being. And the pious householder was enjoined to perform these duties to all beings before he tasted his daily food.

The fourteen Vedic rites, the seven Grihya rites, and the nineteen domestic ceremonies were the forty sacraments of the ancient Hindus, and the object of these sacraments is sufficiently clear. The pious Hindu, wherever he lived, in the vast region from the Himálayas to Cape Comorin, performed the same rites, followed the same customs, and was required to display in his life the same living example of piety, purity, and disinterestedness. And indeed the venerable Gautama, after describing the sacraments, rises to the great conception that true virtue, and not the mere performance of sacraments, leads to heaven.

"He who is sanctified by these forty sacraments, but whose soul is destitute of the eight great virtues, will not be united with God nor reach his heaven.

"But he forsooth who is sanctified by a few only of these forty sacraments, and whose soul is endowed with the great virtues, will be united with God and will dwell in his heaven."

Similarly Vasishtha, another writer of this period, says:

"The Vedas do not purify him who is deficient in good conduct, though he may have learnt them all together with the six Angas; the sacred texts depart from such a man, even as birds when full fledged leave their nests.

"As the beauty of a wife causes no joy to a blind man, even so all the Vedas, together with the six Angas and sacrifices, bring no blessing to him who is deficient in good conduct.

"The several texts do not save from sin the deceitful man who behaves deceitfully. But the Veda, two syllables of which are studied with due observance of the rules of virtue, purifies, just like the clouds in the month of Asvina."

It was but a short step from this to Buddhism, of which we will speak in a subsequent chapter, and which eschewed sacred texts and rites and made *a religion of sinless life*.

We have briefly alluded to the rites prescribed by the Srauta Sútras and the Grihya Sútras. The Dharma Sútras lay down criminal and civil laws which throw much light on the state of society. The caste system had its effect on the administration of criminal law, and the inequality of punishments prescribed for men of different castes is striking.

Four or five kinds of offences were considered heinous,

and were generally punishable with death. To kill a Brahman, to violate a Guru's bed, to drink spirituous liquors, or to steal a Brahman's gold was considered a heinous crime. If a Brahman committed one of these offences, he was branded on the forehead and banished from the country, for *a Brahman could under no circumstances be executed.* A man of any other caste committing one of these offences suffered death.

The same distinction pervades the laws for the punishment of minor offences, and a Súdra who assaulted a higher-caste man was liable to lose the limb with which he made the assault. These unequal laws were not peculiar to India, for the conquerors and the conquered, freemen and helots, patricians and plebeians, barons and serfs, white men and slaves, never had the same laws in ancient or in modern times. It is only within the present century that nations have recognized to some extent the equality of men. No wonder, therefore, that the ancient Hindus also treated the conquered Súdras with undue severity, and that their unequal laws have found a place in their caste rules.

Thefts were visited with capital punishment when the offender was detected in the act, but the king could exercise his prerogative of mercy. The cultivator and the artizan were protected with a tender regard for their welfare, and crimes relating to a cultivator's land or to a mechanic's trade, were punished with the utmost severity.

The civil law of the period deals with rules for leasing lands for cultivation, with damages done by cattle to crops, with the rules of acquiring property and the rates of interest. Property could be acquired in eight different methods, viz., by inheritance or purchase, by gift from a husband or ordinary gift, by pledge, or as consideration for performing a sacrifice, by partnership, or as wages of labour. The ordinary rate of interest for money lent on security was 15 per cent., and interest ceased when the principal was doubled. But where no security was given, a much higher rate of interest was charged, and the principal could be increased six or eight fold.

Such minute and detailed rules show the scrupulous care with which the prevalent customs of the age were settled and fixed. It was, however, on the law of inheritance that Hindu legists bestowed the greatest attention. The birth of a son was not only considered a blessing, but as a religious duty and as a means of salvation; for where there was no heir, there was no one to offer funeral oblations to the deceased. Thus an undue anxiety to leave heirs led the ancient Hindus to recognize various descriptions of children other than those born in wedlock.

In default of an heir being born, a child could be adopted; and if a man died without leaving such heir, either born or adopted, the widow was allowed to raise issue to the deceased. The child of a girl born before her marriage was sometimes recognized by her husband after marriage, or the son of a daughter might be accepted as its grandsire's adopted son, if he had no male issue.

Such and similar kinds of heirs were recognized by ancient Hindu lawgivers; but a reaction soon set in against these rules. A'pastamba, who is one of the latest of the Dharma Sútra writers, explains away the rules laid down by his predecessors, and declares that the son of a man by his married wife was the only description of son that could be recognized. Modern Hindus acknowledge only sons born in wedlock, or adopted sons when no heir is born.

Polygamy was allowed among the ancient Hindus, but was not encouraged. It was allowed specially to ensure male issue. "If a man," says A'pastamba, "has a wife who is willing and able to perform her share of religious duties, and *who bears sons*, he shall not take a second." On the other hand, a woman was allowed to marry again if her husband was insane or impotent, or had lost his caste, or when he was dead.

At the marriage, the father decked his daughter with ornaments, and carried her to the altar. There the officiating priest helped her to offer a sacrifice to fire, and after some other rites she was united to her lord. This was the usual form of marriage, but Hindu legislators noted all other forms of union which prevailed in the times, and legalized them in their codes. A pure love marriage, in which a lover accepted a loving damsel as his wife, was recognized; and the custom, which was prevalent among the lower classes of people, of giving their girls in marriage for a consideration in cattle or money, was also legalized. Kshatriya warriors often carried away a bride after winning a battle, while Hinduized aboriginal races still won their wives by force or by stealth. It is creditable to the catholic spirit of the times that Hindu legislators noticed and recognized all these forms of marriage, although they censured them, and recommended for Aryan Hindus the purer form described above.

Marriages between kinsfolk, *i.e.*, between men and women related within four or six degrees on the mother's or the father's side, were strictly prohibited. Hindu girls married at a proper age in the ancient times, and Vasishtha laid down the rule that maidens should wait for three years after they had attained womanhood. The cruel rite of *Sati*, which permitted widows to perish on the pyre of their husbands, and which came into fashion in later and more degenerate times, was not generally prevalent among the Hindus of this age. To die by the fire is an ostentatious form of suicide, which was known in India from ancient times, and men sometimes committed suicide in this form when grief or suffering or disgrace became insupportable, and the world became cheerless; and among certain tribes of India who were not Aryan Hindus, women sometimes perished on the funeral pyre of their husbands. But this last custom was unknown to Hindus generally in ancient times, and finds no sanction in the ancient Dharma Sútras, or even in later codes of Hindu law which were composed centuries after the birth of Christ.

It may be easily imagined that the Dharma Sútras, which deal so copiously with the laws and rules of society, are not silent on the subject of caste. The expansion of Aryan Hindus over all parts of India suggested or encouraged the compilation of these manuals which were designed to keep Aryan manners pure and undefiled. The same expansion brought the Aryan Hindus in contact with various new tribes and non-Aryan races, who did not belong to the four castes which were known to them. Accordingly, we find the Sútra writers labouring to explain the origin of these races consistently with their theory of caste. That theory was elastic and comprehensive, and so new races and tribes, as they became Hinduized, began to form new castes in the hierarchy of the Hindu community.

Ambashthas, Ugras, and Nishádas, Mágadhas and Vaidehakas, Kukkutakas and Chandálas—all the swarming aboriginal races and tribes of India who came under the shadow and shelter of Hindu civilization and became Hinduized—were provided for and reckoned as separate Hindu castes. Their main occupations or habits were observed and noted, and the Dharma Sútras boldly give us a comprehensive list of castes, with the duties of each caste.

But the Sútra writers went still further. They believed

that in the beginning all mankind was divided into the original four castes, viz., Brahmans, Kshatriyas, Vaisyas, and Súdras, and they laboured to find an origin for new races whom they found all over India, and who did not belong to these castes. The strange myth was then conceived that the new aboriginal tribes were formed by inter-marriages among the parent castes. We may imagine a dogmatic Greek priest of the fifth century declaring that the Huns were descended from a Roman patrician who had married a Parthian maiden; or we may conceive a monk of the thirteenth century laying it down that the Moguls were descended from a German baron who had settled in Arabia and married a maiden of Mecca. Such wild conjectures would be believed in an ignorant age, but would be forgotten with the progress of knowledge. But in India, where the spread of knowledge became more and more restricted in course of time, the ridiculous conjecture of the priests of the Rationalistic Age has been the belief of ages!

The Dharma Sútras of the age thus derive an Ambashtha from a Brahman and a Vaisya female, an Ugra from a Kshatriya and a Sudra woman, a Nisháda from a Brahman and a Sudra woman, a Mágadha from a Sudra and a Vaisya woman, a Chandála from a Sudra and a Brahman woman, and so on! Those who know anything of the millions of Chandálas in Bengal, know well enough that they are an industrious aboriginal tribe, proficient in fishing, boating, and agriculture, and who have become Hinduized as they have come under the influence of Hindu civilization. It is thus that the *race castes* of India have been formed, each aboriginal race forming a caste of its own as it came within the pale of the Hindu world.

It is important to note, however, that the numerous *profession castes* of modern India were not yet formed in the Rationalistic Age. Potters and weavers, blacksmiths and goldsmiths, gold merchants and spice merchants, who all form separate castes in modern India, were still included in the one Vaisya caste of ancient times. Foreign subjection and consequent degeneracy have fostered division and disunion among the sons of the same parent caste, until every trade-guild of modern India is a caste of its own. This division and disunion among the mass of the Hindu people were unknown in ancient times.

CHAPTER III.

SCIENCE AND PHILOSOPHY.

THE adventurous Hindus of this epoch not only carefully codified their laws and social rules, but also achieved a degree of success in the cultivation of science and philosophy which is still more striking and brilliant. The daring spirit which enabled them to cross mountains and forests, and to conquer and Hinduize strange and unknown nations living a thousand miles from their original Gangetic home, led them also to pursue their inquiries boldly in the realms of science and speculative thought. Other nations have carried scientific researches to a higher state of perfection in modern, and even in ancient times, but it is very doubtful if any nation has in any age displayed a higher inventive intellect, or made more original discoveries for the benefit of successive ages, than the Hindus of the Rationalistic Age.

The right pronunciation of words and the correct construction of sentences were considered essential to the proper performance of religious sacrifices, and the constant attention which was bestowed on this subject led to the investigation of the science of grammar earlier perhaps in India than anywhere else. The age of Pánini, the greatest grammarian of India, has been the subject of much learned discussion, and probably the seventh or eighth century before Christ is not an improbable date. He too had his predecessors, but his work is so great and perfect as to eclipse all previous compilations in that science. The great discovery has been made in Europe in the present century that the tens of thousands of words in the Aryan languages can be resolved into a small number of roots. This discovery was made in India, with reference to the Sanscrit language, by Pánini and his predecessors; and his rules of derivation and construction are so perfect, that they have since given a fixedness to the sacred language of India.

The construction of altars also engaged the close attention of the early Hindus, and this led, as we have stated in the last book, to the discovery of the principles of geometry. The earliest rules were no doubt arrived at in the Epic Age, but we find them for the first time carefully arranged and compiled in the Sulva Sútras of the Rationalistic Age. The earliest description of altars was to be 7½ purushas, *i.e.*, 7½ squares, the side of each square being equal to a purusha or a man with uplifted arms. Altars of other shapes, circular or triangular, had to be constructed *without altering the area* of 7½ purushas. At the second construction of the altar, one square purusha had to be added to the area, and at the third construction, two square purushas had to be added, *without altering the shape*. In other constructions, squares had to be found equal to two or more given squares, or equal to the difference of two given squares; oblongs had to be turned into squares and squares into oblongs; triangles had to be constructed equal to given squares or oblongs, and so on. The last task was that of finding a circle equal to a given square. It is needless to remark that all these various tasks required a very considerable knowledge of geometry, and thus the proper performance of religious rites led to the pursuit of that science in India.

Geometry is popularly believed to be a Greek science, and Pythagoras is said to have discovered its first crude rules in the sixth century. But the Sulva Sútras are older than Pythagoras, and the rules framed in the Epic Age are older than the Sulva Sútras; and there can be little doubt from the facts ascertained by Von Schrader and other scholars that Pythagoras borrowed his knowledge of geometrical rules as well as many other ideas from India.

In the science of arithmetic the originality of the Hindus is more universally acknowledged. Decimal notation was not known to the Greeks or the Romans; the world owes it to the Hindus. From them the Arabs learnt it, and introduced it in Europe.

We are unfortunately ignorant of the progress made in astronomy in the Rationalistic Age, as the works of that period have been replaced by more perfect works of later ages. Parásara and Garga are known as the earliest eminent astronomers of India, and the former is said to have lived in the Epic Age, but the works which are now extant, bearing their names, were composed only a century or two before Christ.

In the science of medicine the Hindus attained a high proficiency at an early age, and Dr. Wise has shown that Hippocrates, the "father of medicine", borrowed his materia medica from them. When the Greeks visited India in the fourth century, they found the Hindus proficient in the art of healing, and Alexander the Great kept Hindu physicians in his camp for the treatment of diseases which Greek physicians could not heal. The science is known as *A'yurveda* in India, but the earlier works on the subject are lost, and the two most ancient works which are now extant, and known by the names of Charaka and Susruta, do not probably date before the Christian era.

But it was in the field of mental philosophy and logic that the Hindus of this age achieved the highest results. The *Sánkhya* philosophy of Kapila, whose date is probably the seventh century before Christ, is, says Davies, "the earliest recorded system of philosophy"; and the latest German philosophy of Schopenhauer and Hartmann is, according to the same writer, "a reproduction of the philosophic system of Kapila in its materialistic part, presented in a more elaborate form, but on the same fundamental lines". So little of what is really new in the field of pure mental philosophy has been discovered by mankind in twenty-five centuries.

It is not possible to give any idea of Kapila's system of philosophy within our limits, but his description of the functions of the senses and the mind are so acute and philosophical as to deserve some mention. The *senses* (*indriya*) merely receive impressions. *Sensation* (*manas*) presents the impressions to consciousness; thus a sound may be made within our hearing and we may not know of it unless our sensation is alive. *Consciousness* (*ahankára*) individualizes those impressions as "mine", and the *intellect* (*buddhi*) discriminates them and forms them into ideas. These ideas are for the use of the *soul* (*átman*). In the language of European philosophy, sensation receives impressions and makes them perceptions; consciousness individualizes them as "mine"; intellect turns them into concepts or judgments, and judgments inform the soul. In the poetical language of a Hindu commentator, "as the headmen of the village collect the taxes from villagers and pay them to the governor of the district, as the local governor pays them to the minister, and as the minister receives them for the use of the king; so the sensations having received impressions from the external organs transfer them to consciousness, and consciousness delivers them to intellect, the general superintendent, who takes charge of them for the use of the sovereign soul."

For the rest, Kapila held that both matter and soul are eternal; that the soul is linked with matter, *i.e.*, with the corporeal body, until it attains perfect knowledge, and is finally emancipated. Lastly, Kapila believed, like the writers of the Upanishads, in the transmigration of souls; but his philosophy is agnostic, because he held that God is unknowable by philosophical evidence.

An agnostic system of philosophy did not satisfy the Hindus, and several centuries after, Patnjali added to Kapila's philosophy his own *Yoga* system. Yoga philosophy has little that is original as a system of mental science, but it dwells on the concentration of the mind on the thought of the Deity as a means of final emancipation. In later times the system has degenerated into dark and puerile, and often cruel, rites.

Probably a century or two after Kapila lived Gautama, the founder of *Nyáya*, or the science of logic. He starts with proof and the thing to be proved, and he dwells on various kinds of proof, as perception, inference, analogy, and testimony. What is remarkable in this system is the development of inference by the construction of a true syllogism. An instance of Hindu syllogism is given below.

1. The hill is fiery.
2. Because it smokes.
3. Whatever smokes is fiery, as a kitchen.
4. The hill is smoking.
5. Therefore it is fiery.

It will be seen the Hindu syllogism is composed of five parts, and if the first two or the last two parts are omitted, it becomes a perfect syllogism of Aristotle. It is difficult to suppose that this analysis of reasoning could have been discovered independently both in Greece and in India, and we have little doubt that the first conception of the science was in India, and that, like many other sciences, it was borrowed and perfected by the Greeks.

Kanáda followed Gautama, and started the system of atomic philosophy called *Vaisesika.* The principle of the system is that all material substances are aggregates of atoms. The atoms are eternal ; the aggregates are perishable by disintegration.

These systems of philosophy alarmed orthodox Hindus, and made them anxious for their ancient beliefs and practices. The conservative Hindus accordingly made a stand, and started two new systems of philosophy in consonance with their ancient practices and faith. The *Mimánsá* school insisted on the performance of the ancient Vedic rites, and the *Vedánta* school proclaimed once more the belief in a Universal Soul, which was first inculcated in the Upanishads. To this day the systems of Kapila and Gautama and Kanáda are cultivated only by a learned few ; the Hindu nation believes in a Universal Soul, from which the whole universe has emanated, and into which the universe will resolve itself.

CHAPTER IV.

BUDDHISM.

IT is not only by her philosophy and learning, however, that India has exercised an almost world-wide influence. The intellectual discoveries of the Hindus were no doubt borrowed by the Greeks, and perfected by that gifted nation, and have been handed down as a valuable heritage to the nations of modern Europe. But it was the noble religion of Gautama Buddha,* proclaimed in India in the sixth century before Christ, which may truly be said to have united the nations of Asia as the followers of the same creed. At this day Buddhism numbers five hundred million votaries, or about a third of the population of the earth.

To the north-west of the flourishing kingdom of the Magadhas, an obscure clan, the Sákyas, lived on the banks of the Rohini river, and enjoyed a precarious independence, more through the jealousies of the Magadhas and the Kosalas, who ruled on either side of them, than through their own power. Gautama was the family name of the royal house of the Sákyas, and Siddhártha, a prince of this house, is therefore known as Gautama, and is sometimes called Sákya, from the name of the clan. As the

* Several distinguished men of this age bore the family name of Gautama. We must distinguish between Gautama, the writer of Dharma Sútras, and Gautama the logician, and lastly, Gautama, the founder of Buddhism.

founder of a religion, he is called Buddha, or the "Enlightened".

At an early age Prince Gautama left his royal home and his wife and a new-born child, and became a wanderer and a mendicant to seek a way to salvation for man. Hindu rites accompanied by the slaughter of innocent victims repelled his feelings; Hindu philosophy afforded him no remedy, and Hindu penances and mortifications proved unavailing after he had practised them for years. At last, by serene contemplation he discovered the long-coveted truth; a holy and calm life and benevolence and love towards all living creatures seemed to him the essence of religion. Self-culture and universal love—this was his discovery—this is the essence of Buddhism.

Gautama Buddha was born in 557 B.C., and he proclaimed his creed at Benáres in 522 B.C. He made some converts there, and then went to Magadha, where Bimbisára, the ruling prince, received him favourably. Day after day the pure-souled teacher attracted new disciples by his benevolent and holy life and his lofty code of ethics, as he begged his bread from door to door. Dr. Oldenberg gives us a picture of the holy preacher and his disciples and their daily work. "He, as well as his disciples, rises early when the light of dawn appears in the sky, and spends the early moments in spiritual exercises or in converse with his disciples, and then he proceeds with his companions towards the town. In the days when his reputation stood at its highest point, and his name was named throughout India among the foremost names, one might day by day see that man, before whom kings bowed themselves, alms-bowl in hand, going through streets and alleys, from house to house, and without uttering any request, with downcast look, stand silently waiting until a morsel of food was thrown into his bowl."

Thousands of people left their homes and embraced the holy order and became monks, ignoring caste, and relinquishing all worldly goods except the bare necessities of life, which they possessed and enjoyed in common. Women joined the holy order in course of time and became nuns, and gardens and groves were acquired, and monasteries were built for their accommodation. Religious mendicants of various orders have lived in India from more ancient times, but the system founded by Gautama Buddha was the first *monastic* system known to India or to the world. Monks and nuns, according to his system, lived as united bodies, possessing things in common, and living under the same discipline and rules of life.

But besides those who joined the holy order there were thousands of others who were lay disciples of Buddha. They did not leave their homes or property, and they even remained members of the castes to which they were born ; but they followed the religious tenets inculcated by the great teacher, and recognized his high code of morality. These lay disciples formed the body of Buddhists ; the number of those who relinquished the world and joined the order was, for obvious reasons, comparatively small.

For a period of forty-five years after he had proclaimed his faith at Benáres, Gautama wandered from place to place, made new converts from year to year, and fixed the rules of monastic life, as well as the social rules for lay disciples. Bimbisára was dead, and the powerful Ajátasatru had succeeded him as the king of the Magadhas, and the new monarch was too wise to offend or persecute so widely respected a teacher as Gautama. As he grew old and felt his end approaching, Gautama said to his faithful friend A'nanda, "I am now grown old and full of years ; my journey is drawing to its close ; I have reached the sum of my days; I am turning eighty years of age. . . . Therefore, O A'nanda! be ye lamps unto yourselves; be a refuge to yourselves. Betake yourselves to no external refuge. Hold fast to the truth as a lamp; hold fast to the truth as a refuge."

The last act of Gautama was to share the hospitality of a poor smith who invited him to his house. Soon after this he fell ill and died. It is said that just before his death the trees were in bloom out of season, and flowers were sprinkled upon him, and the sound of music was heard in the air. But the great teacher turned to his friend and said, "It is not thus, A'nanda, that the Tathágata (Buddha) is rightly honoured, reverenced, venerated, held sacred or revered. But the brother or the sister, the devout man or the devout woman, who continually fulfils all the greater and lesser duties, who is correct in life, walking according to precepts, it is he who rightly honours, reverences, venerates, holds sacred, and reveres the Tathágata (Buddha) with the worthiest homage." This was the teaching of his life; this was the teaching of his death. He died in 477 B.C.

The teachings of Gautama Buddha are preserved in the well-known *Three Pitakas*, which are the Buddhist Scriptures.

The works comprised in the Sutta Pitaka profess to record the sayings and doings of Gautama Buddha himself. He is himself the speaker in the earliest works of this Pitaka; occasionally one of his disciples is the instructor, but his doctrines and precepts are preserved throughout, professedly in his own words.

The Vinaya Pitaka contains the rules of monastic life, *i.e.*, of the duties of monks and nuns. As Gautama lived for forty-five years after he proclaimed his religion, there is no doubt he himself settled and laid down most of the rules contained in this Pitaka. At the same time, many minute rules no doubt grew up after his death, but have been incorporated in the Pitaka.

The Abhidhamma Pitaka contains disquisitions on various subjects like the conditions of life in different worlds, the elements, the causes of existence, &c. Much of this has probably grown up after Gautama's death, no doubt on the doctrines and main principles laid down by him.

It is said that in the year of Gautama's death five hundred of his followers assembled at Rajagriha, then the capital of Magadha, and chanted together the teachings of Gautama to fix them on their memory. This was the way in which sacred texts were preserved before printing or published works were known.

A hundred years later, *i.e.*, in 377 B.C., there was a schism among the Buddhists, and there was disagreement on ten points. A second council was therefore assembled, and the disputed points were determined. But the seceders went away in large numbers, and the difference was never healed, but has widened in the course of ages. The Northern Buddhists, *i.e.*, those of Nepal, Thibet, China, and Japan, are the successors of the seceders, while the Southern Buddhists, *i.e.*, those of Ceylon, Burma, and Siam, represent the other side.

Over a century after this, Asoka the Great, then Emperor of Magadha and of Northern India, held a third Buddhist council about 242 B.C., and the sacred texts were once more chanted together by a thousand monks. A son or nephew of Asoka then went to Ceylon and introduced Buddhism in that island, and the sacred texts carried there by word of mouth were reduced to writing in 88 B.C., in the form in which we have the Three Pitakas of Ceylon to this day.

It will appear from this brief history that the Three Pitakas of Ceylon, from which we now derive our information of the teachings of Gautama Buddha, faithfully represent his doctrines and precepts. Those who are aware how faithfully the Hindus have preserved their ancient learning and sacred texts by memory from century to century, how every word, every syllable, every accent of such ancient works as the Vedas have thus been preserved unaltered by generations of men who passed their lifetime in this duty of transmitting ancient texts, and how to the present day, when printing is known, and published books are cheap, the Hindus still learn their sacred texts from generation to generation by word of mouth,—will have small reason for wonder that the teachings of Gautama Buddha were chanted together, and fixed on the memory and faithfully preserved for a few centuries after his death, until they were finally settled at the great council of 242 B.C., and committed to writing in the Pali language in Ceylon in 88 B.C. We may therefore unhesitatingly accept the Southern Scriptures as a faithful record of Buddha's religious teachings.

The works of the Northern Buddhists are generally of a later date, and bear marks of a wide departure from the original teachings of Gautama. Other nations than the Hindus have preserved these works, and they received their first instructions much later than the Ceylonese. Thus Buddhism spread in China from the second to the fourth century after Christ, and in Japan in the sixth century. For an account of the original teachings of Gautama Buddha, it is safe to rely on the Scriptures of the Southern Buddhists of Ceylon. The Hindus of India have long since given up Buddhism and returned to Hinduism, and have therefore preserved no Buddhist Scriptures.

We have stated before that Gautama rejected the Vedic sacrifices, which required the slaughter of animals, and also rejected Hindu penances, which he said were useless. Nevertheless, it would be a mistake to suppose that the great teacher rejected Hinduism altogether, and desired to found a new religion. On the contrary, his idea was to restore the religion of his nation and his country to its original purity, and when he preached Buddhism, he believed he was proclaiming the religion of the Aryas in its pure and original form.

And an examination of his main tenets will show that Buddhism has grown out of the ancient religion of the Hindus. The monastic system of the Buddhists has grown out of the life of ascetics and religious mendicants, whom Hinduism recognized and respected, and for many centuries after the Buddhist monastic system was formed these monks and nuns were regarded by the Hindus as only a new sect of ascetics, among many others which flourished in India. The Buddhist doctrine of *Karma*, which lays down that each act in this life bears its fruit in the next, has grown out of the Hindu idea of transmigration of souls, first inculcated in the Upanishads, and recognized even in the Hindu systems of philosophy. The Buddhist doctrine of *Nirvána*, or the attainment of a sinless state of existence, has grown out of the Hindu idea of final union with the Universal Soul, which is also inculcated in the Upanishads. And lastly, Hindu gods, Brahma, Indra, &c., found a place in the popular faith of the Buddhists, who believed that the gods, as well as men, were all progressing towards the blessed Nirvána, that sinless life which is the Buddhist's heaven and salvation.

Thus founded on Hinduism, the religion of Buddha has ranked as a great religion, and has received its millions of votaries by its characteristic feature—its appreciation of a sinless life above all other things in the universe. This sinless life, this Nirvána, is what gods and angels and men are struggling to attain in repeated births; it is greater than angels and higher than gods; and Gautama

Buddha, therefore, who attained it in life, is the object of veneration of gods and men alike. He is the central figure, therefore, of veneration, and even of worship, and the whole universe of living beings is struggling in different worlds, under different forms of life, and in different circumstances, to attain that which Gautama attained in life. The faith of Buddhists, therefore, points to Buddha as the ideal of life and of religion. The Buddhist loves his brother men ; he recognizes gods, who are fellow-beings striving for the same end ; he respects Bodhisatvas, or saints who have, after repeated births, nearly reached the state of a Buddha ; but his final idea is the state of a Buddha—a state of sinlessness and holiness, beyond which there is nothing higher, greater or holier, and towards which all living beings are marching. The great and striking idea of placing a sinless life, attainable by man by his own exertions in this world, above all the powers and beings of the universe, attests to the loftiness of Gautama's faith in purity and in holiness.

Buddhism is a system of self-culture for the attainment of this sinless state of existence. The Four Truths of this religion are, that life is suffering ; that the thirst for life is the cause of suffering ; that the cessation of this thirst is the cessation of suffering ; and that this salvation can be secured by following the path of duty, the Eightfold path, or Middle path, as it is sometimes called. It is called the Eightfold path because it prescribes right beliefs, aspirations, speech, and conduct, and right living, exertion, thought, and contemplation ; and it is called the Middle path because it avoids sensuality on the one hand, and needless penances and mortification on the other. The rules of self-culture are elaborate and minute, but they need not detain us, as we are concerned here merely with the main principles of Buddhism.

It is by such prolonged self-culture that one can attain

Nirvána, that sinless state of life which is the Buddhist's heaven.

"There is no suffering for him who has finished his journey and abandoned grief, who has freed himself on all sides, and thrown off all fetters.

"They depart with their thoughts well collected; they are not happy with their abode; like swans who have left their lake, they leave their house and home."

"Tranquil is his thought, tranquil are his word and deed, who has been freed by true knowledge, who has become a tranquil man."—*Dhammapada.*

It will appear that the Buddhist's Nirvána is a state of holiness and blessedness in life, not a state of joys and happiness in a future world. The Buddhist Scriptures are obscure as to the hopes of a future life after Nirvána has been attained. The Buddhist does not look beyond Nirvána; no pictures of joys and pleasures in heaven tempt him, no imaginary rewards appeal to his selfish nature. The attainment of Nirvána, of a state of sinlessness, is the final end of the Buddhist's hopes and endeavours.

And if a man does not attain to this state of Nirvána, he is liable to future births. The Buddhists do not believe in the existence of souls, but nevertheless believe in the Hindu theory of repeated births. Their theory is that Karma, or the doing of a man, cannot die, and must lead to its legitimate result in another life; and every pious Buddhist believes that his state of life is determined by his Karma or doing in a previous life. But wherein is the identity of the man who is born with the man who is dead if there is no soul? The Buddhist answers: "In that alone which remains when a man dies and is dissolved into atoms—in his action, thought, and speech; in his Karma, which can never die."

Such are some of the principal doctrines of Buddhism;

but it is not abstract doctrines which attract mankind and unite nations. The charm of Buddhism is in its predominating idea of holiness and in its excellent ethics and morality. The religion is rich in its moral precepts, rich in its instructions, and rich in its legends and parables. The whole of the Dhammapada is a collection of excellent moral rules, inculcating unselfishness and benevolence, love and charity. A few of the maxims may be quoted here as instances.

5. "Hatred does not cease by hatred at any time; hatred ceases by love; this is its nature."

51. "Like a beautiful flower, full of colour but without scent, are the fine and fruitless words of him who does not act accordingly."

55. "Sweeter than the scent of sandal or the Tagara flower, of lotus or the Vassiki flower, is the scent of good acts."

141. "Not nakedness, not platted hair, not dirt, not fasting or lying on earth, nor rubbing with dust, nor sitting motionless, can purify a mortal who has not overcome desires."

183. "Not to commit sin, to do good, and to purify one's mind; this is the teaching of the Buddhas."

197. "Let us live happily, not hating those who hate us. Among men who hate us, let us live free from hatred."

223. "Let one overcome anger by love. Let him overcome evil by good. Let him overcome the greedy by liberality, the liar by truth."

252. "The fault of others is easily perceived, but that of oneself is difficult to perceive. A man winnows his neighbour's faults like chaff, but his own fault he hides as a cheat hides the die from the gambler."

Of the numerous parables by which Gautama tried to impress on his followers love and charity for men, it is impossible to say much within our limits. One instance must therefore suffice, and we select the story of Dígháwu, prince of the Kosalas.

Brahmadatta, king of the Kásís, was rich in treasures, rich in troops and vehicles, and the lord over a great realm. And Díghíti, king of the Kosalas, was poor in treasures, poor in troops and vehicles, and the lord over a small realm.

As often happens, the rich king robbed the weak one of his realm and treasures, and the exiled monarch sought shelter in flight. He had a son born unto him named Dígháwu, and in course of time the boy reached years of discretion.

The retreat of the exiled king was discovered, and he was executed. The dying king looked at his son, and, with more than human forgiveness, said to him, "*Not by hatred, my dear Dígháwu, is hatred appeased. By love, my dear Dígháwu, hatred is appeased.*"

The young son of the murdered father went to the forest and wept. At last he formed the resolution to be revenged for his father's death, and took employment in the royal stables of his father's murderer.

Early in the dawn he arose and sang in a beautiful voice; and his voice was so sweet that the king heard him and employed him as his page, little knowing of his descent.

And it so happened that the king went out to hunt, taking young Dígháwu with him. Dígháwu drove the king's chariot in a direction different from that in which his hosts went. At last the king felt tired and lay down, laying his head on the lap of young Dígháwu.

This was the opportunity which the disguised prince had long sought, and thoughts of revenge rose in his mind. "By him," he thought, "we have been robbed of our troops and vehicles, our realm, our treasures and storehouses; and he has killed my father and mother.

Now the time has come to me to satisfy my hatred." And he unsheathed his sword.

But with the recollection of his father, the last words of his dying parent came to his mind;—"*Not by hatred, my dear Díghávu, is hatred appeased. By love, my dear Díghávu, hatred is appeased.*" The prince would not transgress his father's dying injunctions, and he put up his sword.

And when the king awoke from sleep after dreaming a frightful dream, the disguised prince of the Kosalas told him all. And the cruel Brahmadatta was so struck by the generosity of the boy that he gave him back his father's troops and treasures and realm, and gave him his daughter in marriage.

"Now, O monks," said Gautama after concluding the parable, "if such is the forbearance and mildness of kings who wield the sceptre and bear the sword, so much more, O monks, must you so let your light shine before the world, that you, having embraced the religious life according to so well-taught a doctrine and discipline, are seen to be forbearing and mild."

We will quote one more tale, the real story of Suníta, one of the elders of the Buddhist Church. It will explain how Buddhism came like a salvation to the caste-stricken people of India, and reckoned its followers by the million among the humble and the lowly, first of India, and then of nearly all Asia.

Suníta says of himself, "I have come of a humble family. I was poor and needy. The work which I performed was lowly,—sweeping the withered flowers. I was despised of men, looked down upon, and lightly esteemed. With submissive mien I showed respect to many. Then I beheld Buddha with his band of monks as he passed, the great Hero, into the most important own of Magadha. Then I cast away my burden and ran to bow myself in reverence before him. From pity for me he halted, that highest among men. Then I bowed myself at the Master's feet, stepped up to him, and begged him, the highest among all beings, to accept me as a monk. Then said unto me the gracious Master, 'Come hither, O monk,'—that was the initiation I received."

Such simple parables and touching stories give us a fuller idea of the religion of love which has found favour among thé nations of Asia than could be communicated in volumes.

EPOCH IV.—BUDDHIST AGE.

THE ASCENDENCY OF MAGADHA.
B.C. 320—A.D. 400.

CHAPTER I.

MAGADHA EMPIRE.

A NEW epoch in Indian history commences from the time of Chandragupta, the contemporary of Alexander the Great. As we have stated, Chandragupta was for some time in the camp of Alexander, and after the retreat of the Macedonian conqueror he ascended the throne of Magadha. He united the Punjab and the North-Western Provinces with Behar, conquered back from Seleucus many districts which had been subdued by the Greeks, and for the first time in the history of the country brought the whole of Northern India from the Indus to Behar under one vigorous rule. He concluded a peace with Seleucus, married his daughter, a Greek princess, and received in his court Megasthenes, the ambassador of that Grecian monarch.

Megasthenes remained in India for five years, from 317 to 312 B.C., and from the scattered remains of his writings we can form some idea of the greatness of Chandragupta's power and the system of his administration. Six classes of officers were appointed by the Emperor to superintend the administration of towns. The first looked after industrial arts, for which India has been famous from the most ancient times. The second attended to the entertainment of foreigners, assigned lodgings to them, and kept watch over their modes of life. The third body registered births and deaths, with a view to levy taxes. The fourth superintended trade and commerce, inspected weights and measures, and regulated the sales of the products of each season. The fifth class exercised a similar supervision over the sales of manufactured articles; and the sixth class collected rates on the prices of all articles sold.

Officers were similarly appointed for the administration of rural tracts and villages. They supervised rivers, measured lands, inspected the sluices by which water was let out from the main canals to their branches for the purposes of irrigation, and rewarded huntsmen. They also collected taxes, inspected the occupations of woodcutters, carpenters, blacksmiths, and miners, and also constructed the public roads.

The military officers were divided into six divisions, corresponding to the divisions of the army. The first division was the fleet; the second consisted of bullock trains, transporting engines of war and commissariat supplies; the third was the infantry; the fourth was the cavalry; the fifth related to the chariots of war; and the sixth to elephants.

Arrian gives us a more detailed account of the Indian army. The foot-soldiers carried bows of the length of a man, and rested them on the ground, pressed them with the left foot, and discharged arrows little short of being three paces long, which nothing could resist, "neither shield nor breastplate, nor any stronger defence, if such there be." They also carried bucklers of undressed oxhide about the length of a man. Some carried javelins instead of bows, and swords not longer than three cubits, which they wielded with both hands to fetch down a lustier blow. Each horseman had two lances and a short buckler, and they managed their horses not with bits, but with circular pieces of leather fitted round the extremity of the horse's mouth.

The laws of war were humane, and the peaceful dwellers of the land were never interfered with. "Whereas among other nations," says Megasthenes, "it is usual in the contests of war to ravage the soil, and thus to reduce it to an uncultivated waste, among the Indians, on the contrary, by whom husbandmen are regarded as a class that is sacred and inviolable, the tillers of the soil, even if battle is raging in their neighbourhood, are undisturbed by any sense of danger; for the combatants on either side, in waging the conflict, make carnage of each other, but allow those engaged in husbandry to remain quite unmolested. Besides, they neither ravage an enemy's land with fire nor cut down its trees."

Of the general manners of the people, too, Megasthenes speaks with equal praise. "They live happily enough, being simple in their manners and frugal. They never drink wine except at sacrifices. Their beverage is a liquor composed from rice instead of barley, and their food is principally a rice pottage. The simplicity of their laws and their contracts is proved by the fact that they seldom go to law. They have no suits about pledges and deposits, nor do they require either seals or witnesses, but make their deposits and confide in each other. Their houses and property they generally leave unguarded. These things indicate that they possess sober sense. . . . Truth and virtue they hold alike in esteem."

Chandragupta died about 290 B.C., and was succeeded by his son Bindusára, who ruled for about thirty years, and of whom little is known. Bindusára's son, Asoka the

Great, was viceroy of Ujain and other places during his father's lifetime, and became celebrated as a warlike prince. He ascended the throne of Magadha and of Northern India about 260 B.C.

Inheriting the magnificent empire founded by his grandfather, Asoka added to it Bengal and Orissa, then known as Kalinga. This conquest brought the eastern seaboard of India under the close and immediate influence of the civilization and religion of Northern India. Other countries, not actually subjugated by Asoka, nevertheless owned the suzerainty of the great Emperor. Bactria, Kabul and Kandahar, and the Dekhan as far as the Kistna river belong to this class, as we learn from Asoka's edicts.

But it was not the greatness of Asoka's empire and influence, but his zeal for religion, leading him to embrace the Buddhist faith, and the righteousness and benevolence of his administration, which have made his name known throughout India and all Asia, and justly entitle him to the epithet of "the Great". The conquest of the whole of Northern India by Chandragupta may be compared with the conquest of the best parts of Europe and Asia by Rome, as in both cases distant countries and nations were brought under the same powerful rule and the same civilizing influence and power. This unification of nations paved the way, in each case, for the spread of a new religion, and Asoka the Great's adoption of Buddhism as the state religion of India has often been compared with Constantine the Great's adoption of Christianity as the religion of the Roman Empire.

Asoka inscribed fourteen edicts on rocks in various parts of his vast dominions in the Pali language, which was then the spoken tongue of Northern India. Five such rocks have been discovered, one on the Indus, one on the Jumna, one in Gujrat, and two in Orissa. These fourteen edicts, (1) prohibited the slaughter of animals; (2) provided medical aid for men and animals; (3) enjoined a quinquennial religious celebration; (4) made an announcement of religious grace; (5) appointed ministers of religion and missionaries; (6) appointed moral instructors to take cognizance of the conduct of the people; (7) proclaimed universal religious toleration; (8) recommended pious enjoyments in preference to sensual amusements; (9) expatiated on the merits of imparting religious instruction and moral advice; (10) extolled true heroism and glory founded in spreading true religion; (11) declared the imparting of religious instruction as the best of all kinds of charity; (12) proclaimed his desire to convert all unbelievers on the principles of universal toleration and moral persuasion; (13) mentioned the conquest of Kalinga and the names of five Greek kings, his contemporaries, to whose kingdoms as well as to various parts of India he had sent Buddhist missionaries; and (14) summed up the foregoing with some remarks on the engraving of the edicts.

From a historical point of view, the 13th edict is the most important, as it makes mention of Asoka's Greek contemporaries. In this edict he mentions Antiochus of Syria, Ptolemy of Egypt, Antigonus of Macedon, Magas of Cyrene, and Alexander of Epiros, and adds with satisfaction, "there where the missionaries of the Beloved of the Gods* have been sent, there the people have heard the duties of the religion preached on the part of the Beloved of the Gods, and conform, and will conform, to the religion and religious instructions." Thus, through the zeal of the great Emperor of India, Buddhism was preached on the distant shores of Greece, Egypt, and Syria in the third century before Christ, and

* Asoka calls himself "Beloved of the Gods" in his edicts. The phrase may have been a part of his name or title.

led to the formation of various religious and ascetic sects, and spread among the people those ideas of love and unselfishness and relinquishment of the world which fructified in later times. "Buddhist missionaries," says Professor Mahaffy, "preached in Syria two centuries before the teaching of Christ, which has so many points in common, was heard in Northern Palestine. So true it is that every great historical change has had its forerunner." *

Besides the rock edicts, there are edicts which are inscribed on pillars, and which were published towards the close of Asoka's reign. Two of these pillars have been discovered in Delhi, one in Allahabad, two in North Behar, and one in Central India. Six edicts are published in all these pillars, except in one of the Delhi pillars, which contains two more. In these eight edicts the pious emperor (1) directed his officers of religion to work with zeal and pious anxiety; (2) explained religion to be mercy, charity, truth, and purity; (3) inculcated self-questioning and the avoidance of sins; (4) intrusted the religious instruction of the people to officers of state; (5) prohibited the slaughter of various animals; (6) proclaimed his good-will to his subjects, and hoped for the conversion of all sects; (7) hoped that his edicts and exhortations would lead men to the right path; and (8) recounted his works of public utility, and enjoined the conversion of the people by moral persuasion.

One passage from the last edict will show that while Asoka extended his possessions in India from the western to the eastern sea, and while he sent missionaries to the ends of the world known to him to convert people to Buddhism by moral persuasion, he did not neglect the comforts and the material well-being of the people.

* "Alexander's Empire," chap. xiii.

"Along the highways I have planted Nyagrodha trees, that they may give shade to men and to animals; I have planted out gardens with mangoes; I have caused wells to be dug every half *Krosa*, and in numerous places I have erected resting-houses for the repose of men and of animals." The benevolent and pious emperor died in 222 B.C., exactly three centuries after the date on which Gautama Buddha proclaimed his religion at Benares; and within these three centuries the religion of the lowly mendicant, who begged for his bread from door to door in Benáres and Rajagriha, had been embraced by the ruler of the land, and had become the state religion of India.

The dynasty of Chandragupta (known in Hindu records as the Maurya dynasty, from the name of Chandragupta's mother, Murá) ended about forty years after Asoka's death. Pushpamitra, who was a general under the last Maurya king, and fought his battles against the Bactrian Greeks on the banks of the Indus, founded a new dynasty about 183 B.C. His son, Agnimitra, is famed in Hindu literature, and is the hero of one of the plays of Kálidása, the greatest dramatist of India. Pushpamitra's dynasty ruled in Magadha for over a hundred years, and then another short-lived dynasty ruled from 71 to 26 B.C.

The empire of Magadha was now about to welcome new rulers. The royal houses of Northern India had drifted into a state of feebleness, and the empire which had laid down the law for all India waited for more vigorous rulers. Such rulers came from the south. The Andhra nation had risen to fame and power in the Dekhan many centuries before, and Andhra conquerors now came to Magadha and ruled that kingdom and the best part of India for four centuries and a half, from B.C. 26 to A.D. 430. Throughout this period they held distant provinces under subjection; and we know that they lost Gujrat in the first century after Christ, and reconquered it probably in the third. With the decline of the Andhras in the fifth century after Christ, Magadha ceased to be the leading province in the country, a position which it had held for a thousand years, from the time of Gautama Buddha, and even earlier.

From the time of Alexander the Great, the western frontiers of India continued to be the scene of repeated foreign invasions. After the departure of Alexander, the Greeks of Bactria had frequent intercourse with the Hindus across the Indus, and Bactrian kings sometimes conquered provinces to the east of that river. Menander, a Bactrian king, conquered the whole of Western India as far as the Ganges, and we know from Buddhist records that the invader delighted in controversies with the Buddhist saint and philosopher Nágárjuna. But about 126 B.C. the little Bactrian kingdom came to an untimely end through the invasions of the Yeu-Chi, a Turanian tribe, and the defeated Greeks then entered India in large numbers, and met with varying fortunes in different provinces.

At last the Yeu-Chis themselves entered India. Havishka conquered Kashmir in the first century after Christ, and his successor, the great Kanishka, ruled in that kingdom, and founded an era which is still known as the Saka Era among the Hindus, and which runs from 78 A.D. Kanishka was also a great conqueror, and extended his kingdom from Kabul as far as Gujrat and Agra. He was also a Buddhist of the Northern School, and held a great council of the Northern Buddhists. If the Scriptures as settled by this council had been recorded at the time, we would have had the sacred works of the Northern Buddhists in a genuine and reliable form, as we have those of the Southern Buddhists. But we have nothing left of the work of Kanishka's council except three commentaries on the Three Pitakas. On Kanishka's death his great kingdom fell to pieces, and Kashmir sank again into insignificance.

Gujrat was one of Kanishka's conquests, and after his death that province became independent under a race of foreign kings, who are known as the Shah kings. Nahapana founded the dynasty, probably soon after Kanishka's death, and has left an inscription in the caves of Násik, from which we learn that he delighted in public works of utility. Another prince of this dynasty, Rudra Daman by name, has left us an interesting inscription in which he tells us that he repaired a bridge which had been originally constructed by Chandragupta, the Maurya king, and had afterwards been repaired by Tushaspa, a Greek feudatory prince under Asoka, the Emperor of India. As may be easily imagined, there were frequent hostilities between the Shah kings of Gujrat and the Andhra kings of Magadha and the Dekhan. Rudra Daman boasts of his frequent victories over Sátakarni, the king of the Andhras. A later inscription informs us that the tide of fortune had turned, and Gautamíputra, the Magadha king, had conquered Gujrat from the Shah kings. The dynasty of the Shah kings closed about the same time as the Andhras, *i.e.*, about the commencement of the fifth century after Christ.

In the meantime, a great nation of invaders, the White Huns, had burst like a tornado on Asia and on Europe in the fourth and fifth centuries after Christ. But of them, and of their history in India, we will speak later on.

CHAPTER II.

ARCHITECTURE AND ARTS.

THE earliest specimens of Hindu architecture which still exist belong to the Buddhist period, of which we are now speaking. Architecture in stone, previous to the Buddhist Age, was confined mostly to engineering works, such as city walls, gates, bridges, and embankments. If palaces and public edifices were also sometimes constructed of stone, no specimens of such have come down to us. And it may be safely asserted that the construction of religious edifices in stone was unknown to the Hindus before the Buddhist era, because temples and images were unknown to the Hindus of the pre-Buddhist ages.

It was the spread of Buddhism that led to a sudden and great development in architecture. Under the monastic system, the Buddhist clergy required large edifices for the accommodation of monks and nuns living together; and as the clergy increased in power and wealth, these edifices came to be constructed of stone. The clergy and the laymen also assembled together for the purpose of worship, and this custom led to the construction of churches, also of stone. Pilgrimages to sacred spots formed one of the essential features of the Buddhist religion, and these sacred places were marked with lofty topes constructed of stone and surrounded by stone rails covered with the most elaborate sculpture. Buddhism has long ceased to be the religion of India, but the remains of Buddhist topes and rails, of Buddhist churches and Buddhist monasteries,—nearly all constructed between the third century before Christ and the fourth century after Christ—are still among the finest specimens of Indian architecture.

Topes and Rails.—Among the earliest topes and rails of which traces have been left, those of Bharhut (between Allahabad and Jabbalpur) are the best known, and were constructed in the third century before Christ. The tope enclosed has entirely disappeared, but about one half of the rail remains. It was originally about 275 feet in length, and had four entrances. Processions of carved elephants, lions, and crocodiles, and series of bas-reliefs representing scenes from Buddhist legends, cover the beams. As these are among the earliest specimens of Indian sculpture that exist, we make no apology for quoting the remarks of Dr. Fergusson, the greatest authority on the subject of Indian architecture.

"When Hindu sculpture first dawns upon us in the rails of Buddha Gayá and Bharhut, B.C. 200 to 250, it is thoroughly original, absolutely without a trace of foreign influence, but quite capable of expressing its ideas, and of telling its story with a distinctness that never was surpassed, at least in India. Some animals, such as elephants, deer, and monkeys, are better represented there than in any sculptures known in any part of the world; so, too, are some trees, and the architectural details are cut with an elegance and precision which are very admirable. The human figures, too, though very different from our standard of beauty and grace, are truthful to nature, and, where grouped together, combine to express the action intended with singular felicity. For an honest, purpose-like, pre-Raphaelite kind of art, there is probably nothing much better to be found anywhere."

We next turn to the great tope of Sanchi. Within a small area, ten miles east and west, and six miles north and south, in the little kingdom of Bhopal in Central India, there are no less than five or six groups of topes containing about twenty-five or thirty individual examples. The most famous among these is the one which is known as the great tope of Sanchi, with a base 14 feet high, and a dome 42 feet high, and 106 feet in diameter at the point just above the base. The centre of this great mound is solid, being composed of bricks laid in mud, but the exterior is faced with dressed stones. The rail which surrounds this great tope is a circular enclosure 140 feet in diameter, consisting of stone pillars joined together by stone rails. The rails are covered with sculpture, and four gateways leading to the tope show perhaps the finest specimen of sculpture that is to be anywhere met in India. We quote again from Dr. Fergusson.

"All these four gateways or toranas, as they are properly called, were covered with the most elaborate sculptures both in front and in rear—wherever, in fact, their surface was not hidden by being attached to the rail behind them. Generally the sculptures represent scenes from the life of Buddha. . . . In addition to these are scenes from the Játakas or legends, narrating events or actions that took place during five hundred births, through which Sákya Muni had passed before he became so purified as to reach perfect Buddhahood. One of these, the Wessantara, or the 'almsgiving' Játaka, occupies the whole of the lower beam of the northern gateway, and reproduces all the events of that wonderful tale exactly as it is narrated in Ceylonese books in the present day. . . . Other sculptures represent sieges and fighting, and consequent triumphs, but, so far as can be seen, for the acquisition of relics or subjects connected with the faith. Others portray men and women eating and drinking and making love."

The great tope was probably constructed in the reign of Asoka the Great; the rails were added from time to time, each rail being the gift of a different person, as the inscriptions show; and the gateways belong to the first century after Christ.

Lastly, we turn to the tope of Amarávatí, near the mouth of the Kistna river, and long the capital of the Andhras of the Dekhan. Its date is the fourth century after Christ.

The central tope no longer exists, but the rails still remain and are loaded with ornament. The outer rail is 195 feet in diameter, and the inner rail 165 feet, and between these two was a path for processions. The plinth of the outer rail is ornamented by a frieze of animals and boys, and its inside is more elaborately sculptured—the upper rail being one continuous bas-relief nearly 600 feet in length. The inner rail is still more elaborately sculptured with scenes from the life of Buddha or from Buddhist legends.

There are remains of numerous other topes and rails in India, but when we have considered those of Bharhut, of Sanchi, and of Amarávatí, belonging to three different periods of the Buddhist age, we have a fairly good idea of this class of architecture.

Churches.—The great distinguishing feature of Buddhist churches is that they are not buildings constructed of stone, but caves dug into the solid rock. The external view of European churches forms their distinguishing and noble feature; but of Buddhist churches, excavated in rocks, there is no external view except the frontage, and the visitor enters into the cave to admire the sculpture and arrangement inside.

Nine-tenths of the Buddhist churches which exist are in the Bombay Presidency, because rocks peculiarly fitted for excavation are found in that Presidency.

There are five or six churches in the Western Ghats, all

constructed before the Christian era. In these caves we find architecture in stone slowly evolving itself out of wooden forms. The pillars of the Bhaja cave, which belongs to the third century B.C., slope inwards at a considerable angle, as wooden posts would slope to give strength to a structure; and the cave is supplied with rafters of wood, as a wooden hut would be furnished.

When we turn to the church of Karli (half way between Bombay and Puna), built in the first century before Christ, we find architecture of this class in its state of perfection. The building, says Dr. Fergusson, "resembles to a great extent an early Christian church in its arrangements, consisting of a nave and side aisles, terminating in an apse or semi-dome, round which the aisle is carried. The general dimensions of the interior are 126 feet from the entrance to the back wall, by 45 feet 7 inches in width. . . . Fifteen (pillars) on each side separate the nave from the aisles; each pillar has a tall base, an octagonal shaft, and a richly ornamented capital, on which kneel two elephants, each bearing two figures, generally a man and a woman, but sometimes two females, all very much better executed than such ornaments generally are. Above this springs the roof, semicircular in general section, but somewhat stilted at the sides. . . . Of the interior we can judge perfectly, and it certainly is as solemn and grand as interior can well be. And the mode of lighting is the most perfect, one undivided volume of light coming through a single opening overhead at a favourable angle, and falling directly at the altar or principal object in the building, leaving the rest in comparative obscurity. The effect is considerably heightened by the closely set thick columns which divide the three aisles from each other."

As in the case of topes and rails, so in the case of churches, Buddhist architecture attained its highest perfection about the commencement of the Christian era. In the subsequent centuries it did not improve, but became more ornamental. Buddhism as represented in the latest Buddhist churches is akin to the form of Hinduism of the sixth and subsequent centuries.

Monasteries.—Buddhist monasteries, like Buddhist churches, were not structures constructed of stone, but caves excavated in rocks. The earliest caves are small ones, into which solitary ascetics could with difficulty creep and pass their time in contemplation. But in course of time large monasteries were excavated, with cells for monks and nuns, and large assembly halls in the middle.

Orissa has specimens of small caves like the Tiger Cave, so called because the entrance represents the open mouth of a tiger; and larger caves, subsequently excavated and elaborately sculptured, are also to be found in this province. All these caves are in two ranges of hills, called Udayagiri and Khandagiri, and belong to the centuries immediately preceding the Christian era.

The sacred and flourishing town of Nasik, in the Bombay Presidency, contains three principal monasteries, known under the names of Nahapana, Gautamáputra, and Yaduyasri. An inscription in the first of these buildings shows that it was excavated by the son-in-law of Nahapana, the founder of the Shah dynasty of Gujrat, who ruled about the close of the first century after Christ. It has a hall forty feet square, with sixteen small cells for monks on three sides, and a six-pillared verandah on the fourth side. The second or the Gautamíputra monastery was constructed by the Andhra king of that name about the third century after Christ, and is exactly on a similar plan. The last or Yaduyasri monastery belongs to the fifth century after Christ, and has a hall 60 feet by 45 feet, and twenty-one cells for monks. It has also a sanctuary with two richly carved pillars and a colossal figure of Buddha with many attendants.

But the most interesting Buddhist monasteries in India are the Ajanta caves, belonging to the fifth century after Christ, and possessing a unique value because they contain fresco paintings with a degree of distinctness unequalled in any other monastery in India.

One of these monasteries, known as No. 16, measures 65 feet each way, and has twenty pillars. It has sixteen cells for monks on two sides, a great hall in the centre, a verandah in the front, and a sanctuary in the back. All the walls are covered with frescoes representing scenes from the life of Buddha or from the legends of saints, and the roofs and pillars have arabesques and ornaments. The figures are natural, the human faces are pleasant, and convey the feelings they are meant to express, and the female figures have the softness and mild grace which mark them as peculiarly Indian. Unfortunately, the means adopted recently to heighten the colour of the paintings in order to copy them, and the "destructive tendencies of British tourists", have much spoilt these invaluable specimens of ancient Hindu painting.

Architecture, sculpture, and painting are almost forgotten arts in India. The Hindus, even in their best days, could never equal the Greeks in these arts. The caste system of India divorced intellect and genius from manual labour, and permitted only low caste men to engage themselves in the arts. Displaying much ingenuity and industry, and even elegance and beauty, Hindu art lacks the higher æsthetic qualities of the Greek art; and a Pheidias or a Praxiteles was impossible among the low castes of India, who were alone allowed to engage in architecture and sculpture.

CHAPTER III.

MANNERS AND LAWS.

WE have seen in a previous chapter that the rules of social life were codified by the Hindus in the Rationalistic Age in treatises which are known as the *Dharma Sútras.* The practice was continued in later ages, but the Sutra or aphoristic form was abandoned, and the rules were composed in graceful verse, and are known as the *Dharma Sástras.* A body of rules was handed down from ancient times under the mythical name of Manu, and was recast in verse in the Buddhist Age, and considerably modified to accord with the customs of the age; and this work, known as the Institutes of Manu or Manu's Dharma Sástra, is to this day recognized as the most authoritative code of Hindu laws and rules.

Castes multiplied as new races were Hinduized and came within the pale of Hindu society, and Manu, like others, was at a loss to trace their origin. Accepting the theory that the human race originally belonged to four castes, Manu declared, as the Sútra writers had declared, that the new castes were formed by the intermixture of the parent castes. Chandálas and Kaibartas and other Hinduized aboriginal tribes, still living in India by the million, were thus derived, according to this fanciful theory, from the intermixture of the parent castes. And as foreign nations came within the purview of the

Hindu writers, the elastic theory was boldly extended to them! Thus Manu describes the Dravidians of Southern India, the Kabul tribes, the Bactrian Greeks, the Turanians, the Persians, and the Chinese, as degenerate Kshatriyas!

While the theory of caste was thus extended in defiance of facts, the practical operation of the ancient institution became more and more hurtful to modern progress in knowledge and in arts. The various industrial professions still belonged to the Vaisya and Súdra castes, and industrial progress and developments became difficult as the classes of people engaged in industries were degraded. The same difficulties were felt in Europe in the Middle Ages, but the artizans and cultivators of Europe succeeded after centuries in shaking off the thraldom of knights and priests. In India the rules of caste have perpetuated the difficulties.

Manu's account of the administration of the country is more grateful to us. The income of the state was derived from crown-lands, and was supplemented by taxes. A tax of two per cent. was levied on the increments of cattle and gold, and a sixth, eighth, or twelfth part of the produce of the soil was required to be paid as land revenue. Revenue was also derived from mines, manufactories, and storehouses, and Megasthenes has told us of the royal officers employed in towns and villages, who collected such revenue and fostered agriculture, manufacture, and trade. Manu adds that the king appointed a lord over each village, lords of ten villages, lords of twenty villages, lords of a hundred villages, and lords of a thousand villages; and it was the duty of these lords to check crime and to protect the inhabitants. But the village communities of India, *which are nearly as old as Hindu history, settled all disputes among the villagers themselves, and managed* their internal affairs; and amidst all the vicissitudes of war and the changes of rulers and dynasties, the village community system of India survived until a recent period. It is much to be feared that the excellent system is dying out under the British rule, and its want of recognition of indigenous institutions.

How agriculture and arts prospered under the ancient Hindu system of administration, we know from the accounts left to us by Greek writers. Megasthenes speaks of "many vast plains of great fertility, more or less beautiful, but all alike intersected by a multitude of rivers. The greater part of the soil, moreover, is under irrigation, and consequently bears two crops in the course of the year. . . . In addition to cereals, there grows throughout India much millet, which is kept well watered by the profusion of river streams, and much pulse of different sorts, and rice also, and what is called *bosporum*, as well as many other plants useful for food, of which most grow spontaneously. The soil yields, moreover, not a few other edible products fit for the subsistence of animals, about which it would be tedious to write. It is accordingly affirmed that famine has never visited India, and that there has never been a general scarcity in the supply of nourishing food."

The same intelligent observer has much to say about the manners of the people. He speaks of seven castes, which can be easily identified with the four castes of the Hindus. His *philosophers* and *councillors* were only two classes of Brahmans, viz., those who betook themselves to religious studies and those who accepted employment under the State. His *husbandmen*, *shepherds*, and *artizans* were the Vaisyas and Súdras, who engaged themselves in cultivation, in pasture, and in manufacture. His *soldiers* were the Kshatriyas, and his *overseers* were only special servants of the king.

We have in a previous chapter described the system of education among the Hindus. Boys left their parents, lived under the roof of Gurus and renowned sages, and, after completing their education, returned and married and settled down as householders. Megasthenes gives us the same account. "The children are under the care of one person after another, and as they advance in age, each succeeding master is more accomplished than his predecessor. . . . After living in this manner for seven-and-thirty years, each individual retires to his own property, where he lives for the rest of his days in ease and security. They then array themselves in fine muslin, and wear a few trinkets of gold on their fingers and in their ears. They eat flesh, but not that of animals employed in labour. They abstain from hot and highly seasoned food. They marry as many wives as they please, with a view to have numerous children."

Elsewhere the same writer again speaks of the fondness of Hindus for finery and ornament. "In contrast to the general simplicity of their style, they love finery and ornament. Their robes are worked in gold and ornamented with precious stones, and they wear also flowered garments made of the finest muslin." And Strabo has a passage about the gorgeous religious festivals of the Hindus, which also illustrates their manners and throws some light on the progress of their arts. "In processions at their festivals, many elephants are in train, adorned with gold and silver; numerous carriages drawn by four horses and by several pairs of oxen. Then follows a body of attendants in full dress bearing vessels of gold, large basins and goblets, an *orguia* in breadth, tables, chairs of state, drinking cups and lavers of Indian copper, most of which are set with precious stones, as emeralds, beryls, and Indian carbuncles; garments embroidered and interwoven with gold; wild beasts, as buffaloes, panthers, tame lions, and a multitude of birds of variegated plumage and of fine song."

But such gorgeous processions were not very common among the Hindus until the Buddhists had set the example. Hindus generally performed their sacrifices and their domestic rites on their own altars, by their own firesides, and Manu gives us much the same account of these rites as the Sútra writers from whom we obtained our information in a previous chapter. The only difference is that occasional passages in the work of Manu betray that the ancient customs were changing and the influence of Buddhism was being felt. The writer of the Dharma Sástra, as an orthodox Hindu of the old Vedic school, condemned Buddhism as atheism, and condemned also the worship of images and celebrations in religious temples, which Hinduism was gradually borrowing from Buddhist rites. The orthodox writer still stood up for Vedic sacrifices performed in the homes and on the altars of the worshippers, and indignantly classed temple priests with liquor vendors. But Manu's protests were in vain; Hinduism borrowed the more popular forms of worship from Buddhism, and by the fifth or sixth century after Christ, Vedic sacrifices were rare in the land, and processions and pilgrimages, joyous celebrations at temples, and the worship of images, became the essence of modern Hinduism. Even the worship of the old Vedic gods, Indra, Agni, Varúna, and others, became rare. The Buddhists believed in a TRINITY, viz., *Buddha*, and *Dharma* (sacred law), and *Sangha* (holy order), and every novice professed his faith in the Trinity before he was ordained a monk. Modern Hinduism similarly adopted a Trinity in Brahma, Vishnu, and Siva, and placed them at the head of all the gods of the Hindu pantheon.

We shall speak of these changes in the religion of the

people in our account of the next epoch, in which we shall describe the rise of modern Hinduism as distinguished from Vedic Hinduism. But it was necessary to briefly indicate the facts here to point out the influence which Buddhism was slowly exerting over the orthodox religion of the Hindus, and also to define the position of Manu. He is the last supporter of Vedic Hinduism, of Vedic gods, and of Vedic rites, and he does not recognize the modern Hindu Trinity, and does not approve of the worship of images. But when we come to his successors in the next age, we shall find that they recognize the Hindu Trinity and the worship of images.

The forms of marriage laid down by Manu are the same that we found in the works of the Sútra writers, and, like the Sútra writers, Manu condemns the baser forms. The feeling against the remarriage of widows was gaining in strength, and Manu disapproves of the custom, although he does not prohibit it, and passages in his work show that it was still very prevalent. In the same way, while Manu approves of the marriage of girls at an early age, it is quite manifest, from all we know of the times, that Hindu maidens generally married in early womanhood. It would seem that the frequent invasions of foreigners in this age and the general insecurity of the times fostered the baneful custom of child-marriage, and the custom became a religious duty after the Hindus had lost their independence. The more cruel custom of permitting widows to burn themselves on the pyre of their husbands finds no mention in Manu's Institutes.

The Institutes are divided into twelve books, comprising 2685 couplets. The two longest books, comprising 756 couplets, are devoted to law properly so called. This portion is still regarded as of special importance, and portions of it are still considered authoritative by the courts of India in the matter of civil litigation among the Hindus.

Manu divides the whole body of substantive law under eighteen heads, which are given below :—

1. Debts.
2. Deposits.
3. Sale without ownership.
4. Partnership.
5. Resumption of gifts.
6. Non-payment of wages.
7. Non-performance of agreements.
8. Rescission of sale and purchase.
9. Masters and servants.
10. Boundary disputes.
11. Assault.
12. Defamation.
13. Theft.
14. Robbery.
15. Adultery.
16. Husband and wife.
17. Inheritance.
18. Gambling and betting.

It is not necessary for our purpose that we should make any lengthy remarks on Hindu law under these different heads ; our object is rather to briefly allude to a few facts which illustrate the manners of the people. Under the head of Debts, we are told that the proper rate of interest on security is 15 per cent. per annum, but for unsecured loans a higher rate could be charged ; and we also learn that female slaves could be pledged like other property by persons borrowing money. From some provisions made under the head of Masters and Servants, we know that in India, as in Europe, there was a healthy rule of keeping a "common" or pasture land round every village and town, and cattle were allowed to graze there. The greed of proprietors and the increase in the value of land have led to the almost total disappearance of such lands.

The boundaries of villages were generally marked by well-known trees, tanks, wells, or fountains. Stones, bones, and pebbles were often buried in the earth to mark such boundaries ; and we are told that when a king was unable to determine the exact boundaries between two contending villages, he should make good any possible loss to either from his crown-lands.

Under the head of Assault, and in criminal matters

generally, we meet once again with unequal laws based on the distinction of castes.

The law of Husband and Wife expressly permits the marriage of virgin widows, but disapproves of the remarriage of widows generally. Such remarriages, however, prevailed in the Buddhist Age, and Manu even tells us that if the husband was not heard of, the wife was to wait for a number of years, after which she could, apparently from the context, marry again.

The law of Inheritance is the most important portion of Manu's laws. Brothers divided the father's property, or continued to live under the joint-family system. In the absence of male heirs, the daughter's son could be adopted as one's own son. The twelve different descriptions of heirs who could be considered as sons have been mentioned by Manu as by the Sútra writers; but only the son born in wedlock is considered as a real son, the others are "bad substitutes for a real son". Hindu usage and Hindu law in the present times recognize no kind of sons except such as are born in wedlock or are adopted.

Manu has a separate chapter on Penances. Killing a Brahman, drinking liquor, stealing a Brahman's gold, seducing the wife of a Guru, and association with men who have committed such offences, are heinous sins. Among minor sins, the modern reader will be amused to find such acts as "superintending mines and factories, and executing great mechanical works", showing the low estimation in which manufacturing industry was held by Manu.*

* It is scarcely necessary to add that, in speaking of Manu in the present chapter, we mean the unknown writer who has compiled the existing Institutes from the more ancient rules, now lost, which were handed down under the mythical name of Manu.

CHAPTER IV.

PROGRESS OF SCIENCE.

WE have stated in a previous chapter that Parásara and Garga are named as the earliest of Hindu astronomers, and that the former is said to have lived in the Epic Age. The work, however, professing to contain Parásara's teachings, and known as the *Parásara Tantra*, undoubtedly belongs to the Buddhist Age, of which we are now speaking. It is written mostly in prose, but partly in verse, contains a chapter on the geography of India, and speaks of the Yavanas or Bactrian Greeks in Western India; and the date of the work, therefore, is probably the second century before Christ.

Of Garga we know something more, and he is one of the few Hindu writers who tells us something of the invasion of India by the Bactrian Greeks in the second century before Christ. He could feel respect for the learned among the Greeks, and the following passage of his is often quoted:—"The Yavanas (Greeks) are Mlechchas (non-Hindus or barbarians), but amongst them this science (astronomy) is well established. Therefore they are honoured as Rishis (saints); how much more then an astronomer who is a Brahman?"

In the historical portion of his work Garga speaks of the Sisunága dynasty of Magadha and then of the Maurya dynasty. Speaking of Sálisuka (the fourth king after Asoka the Great) he says, "Then the viciously valiant Greeks, after reducing Sáketa (Oudh), Panchála, and

Mathurá, will reach Kusumadhvaja (Patna). Pushpapura (Patna) being taken, all provinces will undoubtedly be in disorder."

Farther on Garga says, "The unconquerable Greeks will not remain in the middle country. There will be a cruel dreadful war among themselves. Then, after the destruction of the Greeks at the end of the Yuga, seven powerful kings will reign in Oudh." We are then told that after the Greeks the rapacious Sakas became powerful, and we have little difficulty in recognizing in the Sakas the Turanian tribe which first destroyed the Bactrian kingdom about 126 B.C., and then poured into India.

A Hindu writer so rarely speaks of foreigners, even when they invade his country, that the above account of the Greeks and the Turanians in Garga's work is considered a curious and remarkable passage in Sanscrit literature. And it helps us to fix the date of Garga's astronomy, or of the work which is before us, as of the first century before Christ.

Other astronomical works were composed within the Buddhist period, but they have mostly been lost. Hindu writers speak of no less than eighteen Siddhántas or astronomical works, and they are named as below :—

1. Parásara.
2. Garga.
3. Brahma.
4. Súrya.
5. V
   asishtha.
7. Atri.
8. Kasyapa.
9. Nárada.
10. Maríchi.
11. Manu.
12. Angíras.
13. Romaka.
14. Pulisa.
15. Chyavana.
16. Yavana.
17. Bhrigu.
18. Saunaka or Soma.

Most of these works, however, are lost, or have been recast in more modern times. Five of them, viz., Brahma, Súrya, Vasishtha, Romaka, and Pulisa, were recast and compiled by Varáhamihira in the sixth century after Christ, in his famous work of which we will speak in a subsequent chapter. A few words about these five Siddhántas will therefore suffice.

The *Brahma Siddhánta* was not only thus included by Varáhamihira in his comprehensive work, but was recast by another astronomer, Brahmagupta, in the seventh century; and Brahmagupta's work has almost entirely superseded the original work of the Buddhist Age.

The *Súrya Siddhánta* is probably the best known work in Hindu astronomy. But the original work of the Buddhist Age was first included by Varáhamihira in his compilation, and has since been recast several times by later astronomers. Nevertheless, the work as we find it now is a "lineal and legitimate descendant", as Dr. Kern calls it, of the original work. In its present state it is divided into fourteen chapters, and treats of the mean places and true places of planets, of questions of time, of the eclipses of the moon and the sun, of the conjunction of planets and stars, of the heliacal rising and setting of planets and stars, of the phases of the moon and the position of the moon's cusps, of the declination of the sun and the moon, of cosmography, of the construction of astronomical instruments, and of the different ways of reckoning time.

Vasishtha Siddhánta was revised by a later astronomer, Vishnu Chandra. A spurious Vasishtha Siddhánta, a very modern work, exists to this day.

Romaka Siddhánta is ascribed by Brahmagupta to Srí Sena. A spurious Romaka Siddhánta exists, which contains a horoscope of Jesus Christ and some accounts of the Mogul emperors of India, Baber and Akbar.

Pulisa Siddhánta was, Professor Weber thinks, an adaptation into Sanscrit of the astrological work Eisagóge of Paulus Alexandrinus. Dr. Kern thinks the identification of Pulisa with Paulus is doubtful, but he has no doubt that Pulisa refers to some Greek astronomer.

These were the five best known astronomical systems of the Buddhist Age, after those of Parásara and Garga. Their dates may be roughly fixed between the first and third centuries after Christ.

In the science of medicine the Hindus had made very considerable progress when the Greeks came to India in the fourth century before Christ. Nearchus (quoted by Arrian) informs us that "the Grecian physicians found no remedy against the bite of snakes, but the Indians cured those who happened to incur that misfortune". Arrian himself tells us that the Greeks "when indisposed applied to their sophists (Brahmans), who by wonderful, and even more than human means, cured whatever would admit of cure".

The medical science is collectively known as A'yurveda, but unfortunately nc work of a date undoubtedly before the Christian era has come down to us. The writings of Charaka and Susruta are the oldest works that exist; and all that we can say about their dates is that they were probably composed within the Buddhist Age, *i.e.*, in the centuries immediately before or after the birth of Christ.

Charaka's is principally a work on medicines, and Susruta's on surgery. There is much in these works which is fanciful, and will appear absurd to a modern physician; but nevertheless the comprehensive nature of the treatises, and the minute knowledge of anatomy, surgery, drugs, and chemical preparations which they show is remarkable, when we consider their age.

Charaka's work is divided into eight parts, which treat of medicines, diseases, and epidemics, of the nature of the soul, of the organs and their functions, of the body and its various diseases, and lastly, of emetics, purgatives, antidotes, various kinds of injections, &c.

Susruta's work is divided into six parts, and treats of surgical operations, of the symptoms of various diseases, of the structure of the body, puberty, conception and growth, of wounds, ulcers, fractures, and midwifery, and of antidotes and special diseases.

Dr. Royle has shown that the medicinal use of metals was largely known to the Hindus. They were acquainted with the oxides of copper, iron, tin, zinc, and lead; with the sulphurets of iron, copper, antimony, mercury, and arsenic; with the sulphates of copper, zinc, and iron; with the diacetate of copper and the carbonate of lead and iron. "Though the ancient Greeks and Romans," says Dr. Royle, "used many metallic substances as external applications, it is generally supposed the Arabs were the first to prescribe them internally. . . . But in the works of Charaka and Susruta, to which, as has been proved, the earliest of the Arabs had access, we find numerous metallic substances directed to be given internally."

The vegetable resources of India are almost unlimited, and the knowledge of drugs shown in the works named above is correspondingly extensive. Most of them are assuaging and depuratory medicines, suited to the climate of the country and the unexcitable constitution of the people. But the knowledge of surgery among the ancient Hindus was even more remarkable than their knowledge of drugs; and it will no doubt excite some surprise, says Dr. Royle, "to find among the operations of those ancient surgeons those of lithotomy and the extraction of fœtus ex utero, and that no less than 127 surgical instruments are described in their works".

The Arabs had access early to the Hindu works of medicine. Serapion, Rhazes, and Avicenna quote Charaka, and Harun-al-Rashid in the eighth century after Christ retained as his own physicians two Hindu doctors known as Manka and Saleh in the Arabian records.

EPOCH V.—PURANIC AGE.

ASCENDENCY OF KANOUJ AND UJAIN. A.D. 400–800.

CHAPTER I.

KANOUJ AND UJAIN.

THE land of the Kurus and the Panchálas on the upper course of the Ganges had been the foremost in civilization in the Epic Age; and although it declined in political power and importance from the time of the rise of Magadha, it was always considered as sacred and holy in a special degree as the home of pure Aryan Hindus. After the decline of Magadha this land regained its former importance, and a new epoch begins with the history of the Guptas of Kanouj, who became the emperors of Northern India.

This powerful dynasty commenced its rule in the fourth century, and the third king of the line, Chandragupta I. of Kanouj, assumed the title of Vikramáditya, a title which was subsequently assumed by many other kings. Chandragupta's son, Samudragupta, was a most powerful potentate, and we learn from an inscription on a pillar at Allahabad that he conquered all the kings of Northern India; that frontier kingdoms like Bengal, Nepal, and Assam paid him homage or tribute, and that the Shahs of Western kingdoms and the kings of Ceylon sent him offerings.

Samudragupta was succeeded by Chandragupta II., who reigned early in the fifth century, and, like his grandfather, assumed the title of Vikramáditya. He was succeeded by Kumáragupta. An inscription of Kumáragupta's time has been lately discovered,* which informs us that a certain temple was built in the year 439 of the Málavas. There are very strong reasons to believe that this *era of the Málavas* commences from 56 B.C., and is the same era which is now generally known in India as the *Samvat era of Vikramáditya.*

Kumáragupta was succeeded by Skandagupta, another powerful potentate. An inscription of his reign tells us that he ruled the earth as far as the seas, and his fame was acknowledged even by Mlechchas or foreigners. He ruled from about 460 to 480 A.D., and was the last great prince of the line. Buddhagupta and Bhánugupta succeeded, and then the dynasty seems to have come to an end.

The cause of the downfall of this dynasty has been variously conjectured, but it is very likely that the invasions of the White Huns in the fifth century effected their ruin. There can be little doubt that the Huns extended their conquests as far as Central India, and Cosma Indico Pleustes, writing in the sixth century, tells us that the Huns in his day were still a powerful nation in India, holding sway in the Punjab.

While the Guptas were yet ruling in Kanouj and in Northern India, a celebrated Chinese traveller, Fa Hian, travelled through the country, and we may pause awhile and take note of the faithful account he has left us of the state of India in the fifth century. He found Buddhism flourishing at Mathurá on the Jumna, where there were twenty monasteries and three thousand priests.

* By Mr. Fleet.

Southward from Mathurá stretched the Gangetic basin, the *Madhyadesa* or central region of India. "The climate of this country is warm and equable, without frost or snow. The people are very well off, without poll-tax or official restrictions; only those who till the royal lands return a portion of profit of the land. If they desire to go, they go; if they like to stop, they stop. The kings govern without corporal punishment, and criminals are fined, according to circumstances, lightly or heavily. Even in cases of repeated rebellion, they only cut off the right hand. The king's personal attendants, who guard him on the right and left, have fixed salaries. Throughout the country the people kill no living thing nor drink wine, nor do they eat garlic or onions, with the exception of Chandálas only."

Fa Hian then repaired to Kanouj, but has told us nothing of this capital of the Guptas except of its two monasteries. A Buddhist pilgrim himself, he visited the spots in Kosála and Magadha which were associated with incidents of Gautama's life. At Patna he was struck with the grandeur of the architecture and the beauty of the sculpture of the royal palace. And after visiting Gaya, Rájagriha, and Champá, he at last went to Bengal, and remained in the seaport of Támralipti for two years copying Buddhist manuscripts.

From Támralipti he went in a Hindu boat to Ceylon, and thence in another to the island of Java. It is interesting to note from his account that the Hindus navigated the seas in their ships in the fifth century, and had introduced Hinduism into Java. From Java, the pious pilgrim at last returned to his native land of China.

We return from this digression to our narrative. The next king who figures in Indian history after the decline of the Guptas is the celebrated Vikramáditya of Ujayini or Ujain. The victor of a great national war, the patron of all that is best and most beautiful in modern Sanscrit literature, and the subject of endless legends, Vikramáditya of Ujain is to the Hindus what Charlemagne is to the French, what Alfred is to the English, what Asoka is to the Buddhists, what Harun-al-Rashid is to the Muhammadans. Numberless romances have been written in all the languages of India about this national hero, and villagers in all parts assemble to this day under the umbrageous pepul-tree to listen with never-failing interest to the never-ending tales of this mighty hero. Neither Roland nor Arthur is the subject of so much romance literature as Vikramáditya of Ujain.

And in this multiplicity of tales and legends his true history is lost! His age and his very identity have formed the subject of much controversy among historians and antiquarians. His name is connected with the Samvat era, commencing from 56 B.C., and scholars imagined for a time that Vikramáditya lived and ruled in the first century before Christ. And some scholars even question the existence of any Vikramáditya of Ujain, apart from the kings of the Gupta dynasty, who assumed that title in the fourth and fifth centuries after Christ.

We do not propose to enter into this controversy. There can be no reasonable doubt that Vikramáditya of Ujain lived and ruled in the sixth century after Christ, and the poets and writers who flourished in his reign have left their works, which are read and admired in India to this day. The principal grounds on which this conclusion is based are briefly these: (1.) The Hindu historian of Kashmir places thirty kings between Kanishka, who ruled from 78 A.D., and Vikramáditya of Ujain, and this brings down the reign of the latter to the sixth century. (2.) A Chinese traveller, Houen Tsang, who visited India in the seventh century, places the reign of Síláditya I. about 580 A.D., and places

Vikramáditya immediately before Síláditya. (3.) Varáhamihira, an astronomer, who is known to have been one of the "nine gems" or nine literary men of Vikramáditya's court, has left us the date of his work, and lived between 505 and 587 A.D. (4.) And the poet Kálidása, another of the "nine gems" of the court, has left us his works, which undoubtedly belong to the sixth century after Christ, and cannot, from the nature of their contents and style, be referred to the first century before Christ.

All that we know historically about Vikramáditya is that he repelled the foreign invaders of India and killed their king at Korur near Multan. The country enjoyed rest from foreign invasions, and the whole of Northern India came under his enlightened and vigorous rule. The arts of peace flourished, science and literature obtained a fresh start, and poetry and the drama lighted their magic lamp and shed a lustre over this Augustan period of Hindu history. Religion itself gathered strength and life, and modern Hinduism flourished under his fostering care.

The next king of Northern India was Síláditya I., and Houen Tsang informs us that he was inclined towards Buddhism, as Vikramáditya was towards Hinduism. But there was no active hostility between the followers of the two creeds for many centuries in India. Kings alternately favoured the one religion or the other, and made gifts to holy men of both, and often father and son or two brothers were of different persuasions. Thus for a thousand years from the time of Asoka, the followers of the two religions lived side by side in Northern India without any active hostility—a remarkable instance of religious toleration, almost unequalled in the history of the world.

Síláditya I. was succeeded by Prabhákara-Vardhana, and after him came Rájya-Vardhana. This last king was killed in a war with Bengal, and was succeeded by Harsha-Vardhana, who assumed the title of Síláditya II., and ruled for forty years, from 610 to 650 A.D.

This great king once more brought the whole of Northern India under his rule, but failed in an attempt to subjugate the Mahrattas of the south. He was a Buddhist, and celebrated the quinquennial Buddhist festival with great pomp, and invited all the princes of Northern India to be present at such celebrations. Kanouj was now once more the capital of India, and the Chinese traveller Houen Tsang was present at one of these great celebrations, at which twenty ruling princes from different parts of Northern India were present. We will here pause for a moment in our narrative, and take some note of the excellent account of India in the seventh century which the Chinese traveller has left us.

Kashmir was still redolent of the fame of Kanishka, and the Chinese traveller tells us of the Buddhist council held by that king. Mathurá was a flourishing city with many Buddhist monasteries, and the Buddhist celebrations of the place are described by the pilgrim with unfeigned pleasure. "They spread out their jewelled banners; the rich parasols are crowded together as network; the smoke of incense rises in clouds; the flowers are scattered in every direction like rain; the sun and the moon are concealed as by clouds."

Haridvára, near the source of the Ganges, was a great place of Hindu pilgrimage, as it is to this day. Kanouj was a flourishing capital, four miles in length, with a moat around it, and strong and lofty towers facing each other. The climate was agreeable, the people were contented and happy, honest and sincere, and learning was respected. The Buddhists and the Hindus were about equal in number, and lived peacefully, and there were a hundred Buddhist monasteries and two hundred Hindu temples.

It was here that the Emperor celebrated the great Buddhist festival amidst assembled princes and nations. A lofty tower a hundred feet high was erected, and near it was placed a golden statue of Buddha. The whole place from this tower to the king's palace was decorated with pavilions and stations for musicians. A small image of Buddha was daily led forth on a gorgeously caparisoned elephant, Síláditya with five hundred elephants marching to the right, and the king of Assam, who had come on invitation, marching to the left with an equal number of elephants. Pearls and precious substances, gold and silver flowers, were scattered on every side. The statue was bathed, and then carried by Síláditya on his shoulders. Buddhists and Brahmans were alike feasted, and each day closed with learned discussions.

The above account shows that the religion of Buddha had already become a religion of image-worship and of pompous celebrations and displays. Later Hinduism has borrowed these features from Buddhism.

Prayága (now called Allahabad) was a sacred Hindu town, and numerous Hindus came to die at the confluence of the Jumna and the Ganges, to be freed from sins and to be born in heaven. Buddhism was not much honoured here. Benáres was another sacred city of the Hindus, and had a hundred Hindu temples dedicated to the god Mahesvara, while there were only thirty Buddhist monasteries.

Magadha was in a state of decline; the capital cities had few inhabitants, but the towns in the interior were still populated. Pátaliputra or Patna, which had been founded by Ajátasatru at the time of Gautama Buddha, and had been the capital of India from the time of

Chandragupta, was now entirely deserted. Similarly, Rájagriha was in ruins.

Nálanda was the site of the greatest Buddhist monastery and university of India for many centuries, and the Buddhist pilgrim is lavish in its praise. "The day is not sufficient for asking and answering profound questions. From morning till night they engage in discussion; the old and the young mutually help one another. Those who cannot discuss questions out of the *Tripitaka* are little esteemed, and are obliged to hide themselves for shame. Learned men from different cities, on this account, who desire to acquire quickly a renown for discussion, come here in multitudes to settle their doubts, and then the streams of their wisdom spread far and wide." Dr. Fergusson justly observes that what Cluny and Clairvaux were to France in the Middle Ages, Nálanda was to India—the depository of true learning, the centre from which it spread over to other lands.

The traveller found Bengal divided into five kingdoms, viz., Pundra or North Bengal, Kámarúpa or Assam, Samatata or East Bengal, Karna Suvarna or West Bengal, and Támralipti or the southern sea-coast. From Bengal he went to Orissa, where he found the people less civilized, and speaking a language different from the Sanscrit language of Northern India.

The traveller then passed through the countries of the Kalingas and the mighty Andhras of the Dekhan, who had been the first power in India for four centuries. In their country he saw the famous Amarávati tope. Farther south he visited the far-famed town of Kánchi (now called Conjeveram), the capital of the powerful Drávidas.

Turning northwards, he passed through the country of the brave Mahrattas, whom he has given an excellent character. "To their benefactors they are grateful, to their enemies relentless. If they are insulted, they will risk their lives to avenge themselves. If they are asked to help one in distress, they will forget themselves in their haste to render assistance."

In the eastern frontiers of this country the pilgrim saw the famous Ajanta caves. He then visited Málava, the country of Vikramáditya; and the people of this country shared with those of Magadha the highest distinction in India for learning. To the west of them were the Valabhis of Gujrat, who carried on a brisk sea-borne trade and were renowed for their wealth. These Valabhis had founded an independent kingdom in Gujrat, under Bhatarka about 460 A.D., when the power of the Guptas of Kanouj was on the decline, and the dynasty of Bhatarka ruled Gujrat for three hundred years, until the Rajputs came from Southern India, overcame Gujrat about 780 A.D., and successively conquered the great kingdoms of Northern India, as we shall see farther on. But the Rajputs had not risen to power when Houen Tsang came to India, and he found the Valabhis flourishing in Gujrat. After visiting a few other minor places, the renowned traveller left India. The historian of India is grateful to him for the light which his records throw over the arts, manners, and civilization of the Hindus of this period.

Síláditya II., in whose reign the Chinese pilgrim visited India, was an enlightened prince and a liberal patron of letters, and works of merit composed in his court are still read and admired by the Hindus. He died in 650, and the history of Northern India then becomes obscure. The next prince of whom we read was Yasovarman of Kanouj, who reigned from about 700 to 730. The lamp of literature lighted in Ujain two centuries before still shone in India, and one of the greatest poets that India has produced, Bhavabhúti, lived in Yasovarman's court. The king, however, was defeated in a battle by Lalitáditya, king of Kashmir, and the conqueror took the renowned poet Bhavabhúti from Kanouj to grace his own court.

Bhavabhúti is the last of the bright galaxy of Hindu poets who graced this age, and Yasovarman is the last famous prince of Northern India of whom we read. The history of ancient India ends with the eighth century, and the two centuries which followed may be justly called the Dark Ages of India.

For the history of Northern India in the ninth and tenth centuries is a blank. No great dynasty rose to power, no men of letters rose to renown, no great work of architecture was constructed. History is silent over these dark centuries.

But we have indications of what was transpiring. The period resembles the Dark Ages of Europe, which commenced from the fall of the Roman power, and closed with the rise of feudal power. In India, too, the power of ancient and cultured but effete races was swept away during these centuries, and when light breaks in again, we find a new race of Hindus masters of India, the modern Rajputs. By the close of the tenth century the Rajputs were the rulers in Ujain and in Kanouj, in Delhi, in Gujrat, and in the Punjab, and were ready to face the Moslem invaders of India.

The origin of the Rajputs has been a matter of much controversy. Many eminent authorities maintain that they were descended from the Sakas and other invaders of India who poured in through successive centuries, and who settled down in Western and Southern India in ever-increasing numbers. The efforts of the Hindu kings to beat them back may be aptly compared to the last efforts of the Roman emperors and armies to keep back the hordes of barbarians who pressed eagerly on to conquest. For a time the Hindus and the Romans succeeded, but the waves of invasion at last overwhelmed the ancient empires in India and in Italy, and their history is then lost for centuries. And when the darkness clears up, the conquerors of Europe had embraced Christianity and were the strongest supporters of that religion, and the Rajputs, too, had been Hinduized and were reckoned as a new class of Kshatriyas, and, with the zeal of new converts, supported Hinduism and stamped out Buddhism.

For it was in the Dark Ages that religious persecution began in India. Monasteries were demolished, monks were banished, and books were burnt; and wherever the Rajputs became rulers, Buddhist edifices went down and Hindu temples arose. By the end of the tenth century Buddhism was practically stamped out from India, and the work of destruction was completed by the Moslems, who succeeded the Rajputs as masters of India. So complete was the work of destruction, that modern antiquarians, who have collected Buddhist scriptures from Ceylon and Burma, Nepal and Thibet, China and Japan, and all parts of Asia, have failed to glean any valuable texts from India, which was the first home of that religion, and where it flourished side by side with Hinduism for over a thousand years!

But the parallel between the Christian barons of modern Europe and the Rajput barons of modern India does not end here. The new masters of Europe and of India had to fight against the same new power, viz., the Muhammadans. The Spanish knights were opposing them in Spain about the same time that Dahir and other Rajput rulers were opposing them in Sindh; and Philip Augustus and Richard the Lion-hearted were fighting them in Palestine at the same time when Prithu Rai was fighting them near the gates of Delhi. In Europe the Christian barons saved their independence, and ultimately expelled the Moslems from Spain and Austria. In India the Rajputs fought and fell, and the Hindus have no modern history from the twelfth century.

The comparison between European history and Indian history from ancient times through successive ages has enabled us to have a better grasp of the course of events in India. The resemblance is indeed remarkable, and shows how the march of events in different parts of the world is controlled by the same far-reaching but unseen influences and causes. But the parallel closes with the eleventh century. Since then the history of Europe is one of independence, progress, and civilization; that of India is one of foreign subjection, and consequent degradation and decline.

CHAPTER II.

RELIGION AND MANNERS.

WE have elsewhere indicated the slow change which the religion of the Hindus underwent during the long centuries of the prevalence of Buddhism. Image-worship, which was unknown in ancient times, was introduced in imitation of the later form of Buddhism. Temples of worship, which were also unknown to the ancient Hindus, multiplied in rivalry with Buddhist churches. Buddhist processions and festive celebrations were surpassed in pomp by Hindu festivals. The practice of making pilgrimages to holy spots, which was peculiar to the Buddhists even from the time of Asoka the Great, was so effectually adopted by the later Hindus, that holy places of Hindu pilgrimage multiplied all over India and drew millions of devout men and women from year to year. And lastly, as every Buddhist professed his faith in a Trinity, so the Hindus of this later age conceived a Hindu Trinity, and paid their worship to Brahma, Vishnu, and Siva, the supreme deities of later Hinduism.

The religion was so changed, in its outward form at least, that the faith and observances of the modern Hindus seem to have little in common with those of their ancestors of the pre-Buddhist age; and in speaking of the Hindu religion, it is necessary to distinguish between early or Vedic Hinduism and later or Puranic Hinduism. But nevertheless the Hindus have never been disloyal to their past, and every scholar knows that in cardinal doctrines there is little difference between these two forms of the faith.

Both Vedic Hinduism and Puranic Hinduism recognize one great God, the all-pervading Breath, the universal Soul of the Upanishads. Both teach that the universe is an emanation from him and will resolve into him. Both recognize rewards and punishments in after life or lives, according to deeds performed in this life, and both insist on the final absorption of our souls in the Deity. In these great doctrines there has been no change and no falling off.

But these are doctrines comprehended only by the learned. The multitude believe in forms and practise observances, and it is here that the difference is marked. The Vedic Hindu worshipped the Deity in the manifestations of nature, in Indra or Varuna, in Agni or Súrya. The Puranic Hindu worships the same great Deity in his threefold power of creation, preservation, and destruction under the names of Brahma, Vishnu, and Siva, and also in a multiplicity of humbler gods and goddesses whose legends fill his sacred works and his imagination. The Vedic Hindu performed his worship by sacrifices at his own fireside. The Puranic Hindu worships images in shrines and temples, or repairs on holy pilgrimages to earn merit.

It is by these changes, these adaptations from Buddhism, these appeals to the popular mind and the popular feelings, that Hinduism finally supplanted Buddhism in India. Priests and rulers could not have won back the millions of India from Buddhist celebrations, Buddhist pilgrimages, and from Buddhist forms of public worship without offering to them equally attractive celebrations and pilgrimages and methods of public worship. This was not intentionally done, but the bent of the people's mind and the practices and observances of the million shaped the new form of Hinduism, and Hinduism remained the surviving religion of India by adapting itself to the popular desire for pomp and ceremony, for public observances and joyous celebrations.

Thus Buddhism effected a great change in the manners and religion of the Hindus. The pre-Buddhist Hindus were always a handful, or a number of handfuls, living among millions of Súdras and aborigines. They naturally adhered, therefore, to the forms of sacrifice which they had brought with them, and on which they set a special value. Before the rise of Magadha the Hindus were only a number of colonist tribes on the Ganges, and they proudly rejected all innovations which affected their cherished and ancient rites. But the rise of Magadha, which brought all Northern India under the rule of a nation not purely Aryan, was the first great blow to ancient and Aryan Hinduism, and made the spread of Buddhism possible. Gautama Buddha himself found more followers in non-Aryan Magadha than in Aryan Benáres; and in subsequent centuries the religion spread from Magadha to Bengal, Orissa, and other non-Aryan provinces to a greater extent than in the Gangetic valley of Northern India. And the spread of Buddhism all over India greatly effaced the distinctions between Aryan and non-Aryan castes, broke down barriers, levelled differences, and tended to fuse tribes and races into a great Hindu nation. One common religion was offered to them all, and in course of time that religion shaped itself to the needs and requirements of the masses, and sanctioned popular celebrations and pilgrimages and image-worship. Hinduism, which flourished side by side, necessarily underwent the same change, and when at last it replaced Buddhism, the change was complete, and Hinduism was a religion of the people,—a religion of celebrations and image-worship.

We have described this change at some length, because the relations between Vedic Hinduism, Buddhism, and Puranic Hinduism have not, so far as we are aware, been popularly explained; and while the changes in religious rites are noted, their causes are left in obscurity. There is nothing obscure in a nation's history if we studiously and carefully note the progress of the nation's mind.

The books which inculcate this new form of Hinduism, and which have given their name to the age and its religion, are known as the eighteen *Puránas.* A class of compositions called Puránas or Itihasa-Puránas, handing down ancient legends and historical narratives, existed from the Epic Age, and are often alluded to in the literature of that age. But these ancient works have been replaced by more modern compositions, until no trace of the older writings is left. The Puránas which are still extant were composed in the age of Vikramáditya and Síláditya, but have been considerably altered and largely added to in succeeding centuries, even after the conquest of India by the Muhammadans. While, therefore, they present to us the main features of the religion of the Vikramádityan era, they reflect still more prominently the sectarian disputes of later ages, when some particular deity like Krishna or Siva became prominent among the gods and claimed millions of worshippers among the Hindus. We accordingly find the Puránas filled with sectarian disputes, each sect upholding the supremacy of its own special deity, chosen from the copious storehouse of the modern Hindu pantheon. As an account of the religion and manners of the Vikramádityan age, the Puránas in their present shape must be received with caution. They present to us rather the religion and customs of the Hindus after the Muhammadan conquest, and even contain descriptions of temples which were built in different parts of India one or two centuries ago!

These remarks apply with still greater force to the modern *Dharma Sástras.* The great work of Manu was the standard and authoritative work for all Hindus for centuries; but as Hinduism changed its form, as Vedic sacrifices went out of fashion and image-worship was introduced, the composition of new Dharma Sástras became necessary. The work of Yájnavalkya * belongs to the fourth or fifth century after Christ, and is the only one which we can with confidence assign to the Vikramádityan age. All the other later Dharma Sástras, like those of Vyása or Parásara,† were composed or recast after the Muhammadan conquest, and give us a picture of the manners of the Hindus under Muhammadan rule, not of the Hindus of the Vikramádityan age.

We have spoken of the Puránas and the Dharma Sástras, which have been composed or so altered since the Muhammadan conquest as scarcely to be safe guides to the historian of the age of Vikramáditya and Síláditya. There is yet another class of religious compositions, the *Tantras*, composed by a particular sect of people who worshipped the consort of Siva. They prescribe dark and sometimes cruel practices for the acquisition of supernatural powers, and are evidently the productions of a very recent age, when the Hindus had ceased to be a free nation. Ignorance is credulous, and feebleness hankers after power, and men in these later times sought by dark and unholy practices to acquire

* Who must not be confounded with the priest of Janaka of Videha, who lived in the Epic Age.

† These must not be confounded with Vyása, the compiler of the Vedas, or Parásara, the ancient astronomer. Later Hindu writers wrote under the disguise of ancient names to give to their modern works an appearance of antiquity and authority. Thus all the eighteen modern Puránas profess to be the works of Vyása, the compiler of the Vedas!

that power which their ancestors attained by a free and healthy exercise of their faculties.

We turn from these compositions, the Dharma Sástras, the Purános, and the Tantras, to the works of genius of the age of Vikramáditya and Síláditya, the works of the poets, dramatists, and novelists of the age, which faithfully reflect the religion and the manners of the times. And the picture we get from these sources is both interesting and pleasing.

The Deity was worshipped in his threefold power of creation, preservation, and destruction. The Creator was worshipped under the ancient name of Brahma, who in the Veda was the god of prayers; and the Vedic goddess of speech, Sarasvatí, was appropriately imagined to be his consort. Vishnu was the sun-god of the Rig Veda, and that name was appropriately chosen to designate the Preserver, and his consort was Lakshmí, the goddess of harvests and wealth. And lastly, Rudra was the thunder-god of the Rig Veda, and that name was appropriately chosen for the Destroyer, who was also called Siva or Mahesvara. Umá, the daughter of the Himálayas, was the amiable consort of the dread destroyer, and she was also worshipped as Durgá and Kálí and Saktí, and under various other names.

The other ancient gods of the Rig Veda, Indra, Agni, Varuna, Súrya, Váyu, Maruts, &c., were considered as minor gods, peopling the luxurious heaven of Indra, contending with Asuras or Titans to keep their celestial empire safe, and occasionally invoking the aid of one of the great gods, Brahma, or Vishnu, or Siva, when beaten by the Asuras. The idea is that the minor gods have attained their rank as celestials by austere penances, and will enjoy the felicity only for a fixed period; that mortals may also by the same means rise to the dignity of gods for fixed periods; that our work brings its reward and punishment in this manner in subsequent lives; and that nothing really endures for ever except the great Deity, who is Brahma and Vishnu and Siva, and into whom all the universe will be absorbed. It was thus that the monotheism of the Upanishads and the ancient belief in transmigration of souls were harmonized with the polytheism of later days.

One of the most beautiful creations of Vikramáditya's age is a poem by Kálidása, which describes the marriage of Siva. The minor gods have been worsted in battle with the Asuras or Titans, and have been expelled from their heaven of felicity. They come, humble and disconsolate, to the great Brahma to seek his all-powerful aid. The great Deity will not help one class of created beings against another, but indicates the way in which the gods can reconquer heaven. The gods want a leader, and Brahma gives them to understand that only a son of Siva can lead them to victory. The great Siva is then absorbed in contemplation amidst the rocks and forests of the Himálayas, and Umá, the daughter of the mountain, attends on him as a hand-maiden. The god of love is despatched by the council of gods to awaken a passion for the mountain maid in the breast of the mighty Siva, but the act, alas, is ill advised! Siva feels the shaft of love, but suppresses his feelings, and in his anger reduces the god of love to ashes!

Umá then repairs to solitary wilds and engages in penances. After months passed in severe austerities, she meets a young anchorite, who tries to dissuade her from the penances unsuited to her age and her sex, and even ridicules Siva, for whose sake she practises these austerities. Umá turns away in anger, but the youth restrains her by gentle force, and the blushing maiden finds in him Siva himself in disguise! Marriage follows, and their son, Kártikeya, leads back the gods to victory and to heaven. A tale like this gives us a clearer and truer idea of the religious beliefs and feelings of the people than volumes of professedly religious works.

Other works of the poets of the age give us an insight into the manners of the people. They were still divided into the four primitive castes, the Brahmans, Kshatriyas, Vaisyas, and Súdras, but various aboriginal races had now become Hindus, and had formed new castes or "mixed castes," as has been already stated. Yájnavalkya enumerates thirteen such castes, but the modern *profession castes* of India, the weavers, the potters, the blacksmiths, the goldsmiths, the physicians, and the clerks, find no mention in this list. The different professions apparently did not form separate castes in the days of Hindu independence; the work of separation and disunion was completed after the Hindus had ceased to be a free nation.

Women in India were still allowed a degree of freedom which they have lost since the loss of Hindu independence. Heroines of dramas, poems, and works of fiction are represented as remaining still unmarried in their youth, resorting to temples without any attempt at concealment, receiving strangers with courtesy, and not running away to hide themselves, and in every respect exerting their proper influence on the society in which they live and move. Married women receive their husbands' friends, and speak with them without any restriction, and not unoften receive guests in their houses in the absence of the male members. Women in the East were never allowed the degree of liberty in their intercourse with men which marks the manners of modern Europe, but in the voluminous Hindu literature of the Puranic Period we do not come across a single instance of a Hindu woman kept in the absolute and unhealthy seclusion in which women in India have been kept since the Muhammadan conquest.

Girls learned to read and to write; singing was considered a female accomplishment, and painting and music were often taught. Marriage was arranged by the parents of the parties, and the ceremony of marriage continued essentially the same as in ancient days, and as it continues to the present day among Hindus. Widows were still allowed to remarry, although this custom was looked upon with disfavour. The cruel *sati* rite, permitting widows to burn themselves on the funeral pyre of their husbands, finds no sanction in ancient Sanscrit literature, not even in Yájnavalkya's work, belonging to the fourth or fifth century.

Domestic slaves were bought and sold in India as in every ancient country, and probably most domestic servants were slaves; but slaves could obtain their manumission by payment of a sum which was fixed as the price of their liberty.

A realistic drama of this period gives us a very clear account of the city of Ujain in its palmy days. Brahman judges dispensed justice according to the Hindu law, with the help of a provost and a scribe, and the police watched the town by day and by night. Gambling-houses and grog-shops were to be found in every town, and the vices of modern civilization were not unknown in ancient days.

India was famed in the past for her rich fabrics and precious stones, and we have an account in the dramatic work alluded to above of a wealthy house where "skilful artists examine pearls, topazes, sapphires, emeralds, rubies, the lapis-lazuli, coral, and other jewels; some set rubies in gold, some work gold ornaments on coloured threads, some string pearls, some grind the lapis-lazuli, some pierce shells, and some cut corals. Perfumers dry the saffron bags, shake the musk bags, express the sandal juice and compound essences."

We also get some account of Indian towns and of the Indian people of this age from the writings of the Chinese traveller Houen Tsang. Towns were generally walled and had gates, but the streets and lanes were tortuous. Stalls were arranged on both sides of the road with appropriate signs, but butchers, fishers, dancers, executioners, and scavengers had their abodes outside the city. The town walls were of bricks and tiles, and the houses of the ordinary people were covered with rushes or dry branches or tiles or boards.

Rice and wheat were the food of the common people; cakes of corn and various preparations of milk were commonly made, and fish, mutton, and deer were also taken. Gold, silver, copper, white jade, and pearls were the products of the country, and there was an abundance of rare gems and precious stones. Commercial transactions, says Houen Tsang, were carried on by barter. Gold and silver coins were not generally used as current money.

And lastly, with regard to the common people, Houen Tsang remarks, "Although they are naturally light-minded, yet they are upright and honourable. In money matters they are without craft, and in administering justice they are considerate. They dread the retribution of another state of existence, and make light of the things of the present world. They are not deceitful or treacherous in their conduct, and are faithful to their oaths and promises."

CHAPTER III.

ARCHITECTURE AND ARTS.

WORSHIP in public temples and ecclesiastical edifices was not a part of the Hindu religion before the spread of Buddhism, and the earliest Hindu temples of India, therefore, date from the time of the rise of modern Hinduism. The province of Orissa was not conquered by the Moslems till the sixteenth century, and the temples of Orissa are the purest specimens of the *Northern Indian style.* These temples consist generally of a high tower and a separate edifice or porch in front. The high tower, rising from a square base, is curvilinear, and is one massive and imposing structure, without any division into storeys, or pillars or pilasters anywhere. The porch, on the other hand, has a conical top with a series of cornices.

Such are the far-famed temples of Bhuvanesvara in Orissa, built in the sixth and seventh centuries after Christ. Several hundreds of stone temples are said to have been erected in this proud capital of Orissa, and numerous specimens still exist, of which the Great Temple is the most conspicuous. The tower rises from a square of about 70 feet to a height of 180 feet, and the whole of the exterior is covered with the most elaborate carving and sculpture work, which is estimated to have cost three times as much as the erection of the building itself. "Most people," says Fergusson, "would be of opinion that a building four times as large would produce a greater and more imposing effect: but this is not the way a Hindu ever looked at the matter. Infinite labour bestowed on every detail was the mode in which he thought he could render his temple most worthy of the Deity; and whether he was right or wrong, the effect of the whole is certainly marvellously beautiful."

As Siva-worship and the town of Bhuvanesvara declined in Orissa, the worship of Vishnu, or his incarnation Krishna, became more popular, and the great temple of Jagannátha was erected to this deity at Puri in the twelfth century. The temple is 192 feet high, and is considered one of the holiest in India to this day, but does not pretend to the architectural beauty of the Bhuvanesvara temples of an earlier age. Orissa boasts of yet another celebrated temple, the well-known "Black Pagoda" of Kanarak, built on the seashore. It is generally supposed to have been erected in the thirteenth century, but Dr. Fergusson would assign to it an earlier date. The porch alone remains, and rises on a square of 40 feet, and the roof slopes inwards till it contracts to about 20 feet, where it was ceiled with one flat stone roof supported by wrought iron beams, 21 or 23 feet long, showing a knowledge of forging iron which has been lost to the Hindus since. The exterior is carved with infinite beauty and variety on all the twelve faces.

As we proceed westwards from Orissa, we meet specimens of the Northern Indian style of architecture in other provinces of India. Bandelkhand, which long remained an independent Hindu kingdom, is rich in Hindu temples, and there are no less than thirty great temples in Khajuraho town alone, belonging to the tenth and eleventh centuries after Christ. The lofty tower of the principal temple is surrounded by smaller towers on all sides; the basement is high, and is surrounded by three rows of sculptured figures, and General Cunningham counted here not less than 872 statues, mixed up with a profusion of vegetable forms and conventional details.

Malwa, which long struggled against the Moslems to

retain its independence, boasts of a perfect example of a Hindu temple of the eleventh century in Bhopal; and farther to the south, the Mahratta country also contains specimens of ancient temples, which are chiefly interesting as exhibiting a mixture of the Northern and Southern styles of architecture.

While thus we meet with specimens of Hindu architecture of the sixth to the twelfth century in Orissa, in Bandelkhand, in Bhopal, and in Maháráshtra, it is remarkable that there are no such ancient specimens in the home of the Hindu Aryans, *i.e.*, in Northern India between the Indus and the Brahmaputra. The reason is obvious. The Moslems conquered this wide tract of country about the close of the twelfth century, and ruled it for nearly six centuries. Ancient Hindu temples in Northern India were demolished by these conquerors, and the stones of those edifices were used to erect mosques and minars. The destruction has been so complete that no ancient Hindu temple has survived in these parts. The existing temples of Benáres, Mathurá, Vrindávana, Amritsar, and other places of Northern India are not over a few centuries old.

When we turn to the south, we find the *Southern Indian style* of architecture entirely distinct from the Northern style, and the best specimens of the Southern style show that it has grown out of the Buddhist style of excavating caves. Accordingly the earliest specimens of the Southern Hindu temples were excavated, not erected, and in their latest developments the Southern edifices still bore marks of their origin.

The excavated temples of Ellora, belonging to the eighth or ninth century, are considered as one of the wonders of the world. An extensive pit, 270 feet by 150 feet, is excavated in the solid rock, and in the centre of this rectangle stands the temple with a tower 80 to 90 feet high, a large porch supported by sixteen columns, and a detached porch connected by a bridge and a gateway. It is a model of a complete structural temple, but carved out of solid rock, and the monolithic character of these vast edifices gives to them an air of solidity, strength, and grandeur. Each of the seven surrounding cells (constructed in imitation of the cells in Buddhist monasteries) is devoted to a separate Hindu deity.

One of the most venerated temples of Southern India is that of Chillambaram, near the mouths of the Káveri river. It was originally constructed in the tenth or eleventh century, but the most imposing edifices belonging to it have been added in later centuries. The great gateways, for instance, and the "Hall of a Thousand Columns" were constructed only a few centuries ago; for the Hindus of Southern India retained their independence down to the last century. The columns are arranged twenty-four in front and forty-one in depth, and this forest of granite pillars, each of a single stone, and all more or less carved and ornamented, produces a marvellous effect. The other great temples of the South, as at Conjeveram (Kánchí), Tanjore, and Madura, belong to a later epoch.

We have still to speak of the *Dekhan style* of architecture, which is different alike from the Northern Indian and the Southern Indian style. Its peculiar feature is that the temples have a polygonal or star-shaped base; the walls rise perpendicular to some height, and then the roof is pyramidical, and tapers to a point.

The Ballala Rajputs, who ruled in the Karnatic from the eleventh to the commencement of the fourteenth century, have left us three remarkable groups of temples in this style. The first is at Somnathapur, built in the eleventh century; the second at Baillur, built in the twelfth; and the third is at Hallabid, constructed in the thirteenth century, and not yet completed when the Muhammadans crushed the Ballala dynasty.

Dr. Fergusson makes some very thoughtful remarks

based on a comparison of this temple with the Parthenon of Greece, and as, although the date of this temple is later than the Puránic age, these remarks illustrate the pervading and continuing spirit of Hindu art, we make some extracts.

"The Parthenon is the best example we know of pure refined intellectual power applied to the production of an architectural design. Every part and every effect is calculated with mathematical exactness, and executed with a mechanical precision that never was equalled. . . . The sculpture is exquisitely designed to aid the perfection of the masonry, severe and god-like, but with no condescension to the lower feelings of humanity.

"The Hallabid temple is the opposite of all this. It is regular, but with a studied variety of outline in plan, and even greater variety in detail. All the pillars of the Parthenon are identical, while no two facets of the Indian temple are the same; every convolution of every scroll is different. No two canopies in the whole building are alike, and every part exhibits a joyous exuberance of fancy, scorning every mechanical restraint. All that is wild in human faith or warm in human feeling is found portrayed on these walls; but of pure intellect there is little, less than there is of human feeling in the Parthenon. . . .

"For our purpose, the great value of the study of these Indian examples is that it widens so immensely our basis for architectural criticism. It is only by becoming familiar with forms so utterly dissimilar from those we have hitherto been conversant with that we perceive how narrow is the purview that is content with one form or one passing fashion. By rising to this wider range, we shall perceive that architecture is as many-sided as human nature itself, and learn how few feelings and how few aspirations of the human heart and brain there are that cannot be expressed by these means."

CHAPTER IV.

SCIENCE AND LITERATURE.

THE closing chapter of this brief history of ancient India will be appropriately devoted to an account of the literature of the Vikramádityan age, which is still studied in India with ardour and admiration, and which still connects modern Hindus in ideas and sentiments and feelings with their ancestors of past ages.

Astronomy, in which considerable progress was made in the Buddhist Age, as we have seen in a previous chapter, received a fresh start in the Puránic Age. The great A'ryabhatta was born in Pátaliputra, the ancient capital of Magadha, in 476, and wrote his celebrated work, known as the *A'ryabhattíya*, after his own name, early in the sixth century. He maintained the theory of the revolution of the earth on its own axis, and explained that "as a person in a vessel, while moving forward, sees an immovable object moving backward, in the same manner do the stars, though immovable, seem to move daily". A'ryabhatta also explained the true causes of solar and lunar eclipses and other heavenly phenomena, and his estimate of the earth's circumference is not very wide of the mark.

His successor, Varáhamihira, was born in Ujain about 505, and he is still popularly remembered in India as one of the "nine gems" of Vikramáditya's court. As we have stated in a previous chapter, he compiled together five of the old Siddhántas or systems of astronomy in his great work known as the *Pancha Siddhántika;* and he also wrote the *Brihat Sanhitá*, a comprehensive work, dealing not only with the sun, moon, earth, and planets, and celestial and atmospheric phenomena, but also with various other matters like images, temples, architecture, animals, precious stones, vegetable products, and manufactures.

Varáhamihira was followed by Brahmagupta, who recast one of the old Siddhántas under the name of *Brahmasphuta Siddhánta.* The date of the work is 628. After this the Dark Ages set in in Northern India, and we have no great name in astronomy until Bháskará-chárya rose in the twelfth century, *i.e.*, in the age of the Rajput revival.

The Hindu writers on astronomy seldom failed to treat of algebra and arithmetic in their works, and the remarks made by the eminent scholar Colebrooke on the progress of Hindu algebra deserve to be quoted. "The Hindus," he says, "had certainly made distinguished progress in the science so early as the century immediately following that in which the Grecians taught the rudiments of it. The Hindus had the benefit of a good arithmetical notation, the Greeks the disadvantage of a bad one. Nearly allied as algebra is to arithmetic, the invention of the algebraic calculus was more easy and natural where arithmetic was best handled. No such marked identity of the Hindu and Diophantine systems is observed as to demonstrate communication. They are sufficiently distinct to justify the presumption that both might be invented independently of each other."

Arabian writers translated Hindu works on algebra in the eighth century, and Leonardo of Pisa learnt the science from the Arabians, and introduced it in modern Europe. In arithmetic, also, the Arabians learnt from the Hindus, and introduced in Europe that decimal system of notation which is now the property of the human race.

It is not, however, for the progress made in mathematics and in science that the age of Vikramáditya is still remembered with pride by the Hindus of modern days. Poetry has shed a lustre on the age, and the immortal creations of fancy belonging to this age made it truly the Augustan era of Sanscrit literature.

The era opens with that gifted son of the Muses, Kálidása, the illustrious poet of Vikramáditya's court. His great dramatic work, *Sakuntalá*, was translated into English by Sir William Jones a century ago, and for the first time roused the attention of the literary men of Europe to the value and beauty of Sanscrit literature; and the greatest literary genius of the modern age has expressed his appreciation of the work in beautiful lines, which have often been quoted in original and in translation :—

"Wouldst thou the life's young blossoms and the fruits of its decline,
And all by which the soul is pleased, enraptured, feasted, fed?
Wouldst thou the earth and heaven itself in one sweet name combine?
I name thee, O Sakuntala, and all at once is said."—GOETHE.

Sakuntalá is well known to English readers, and it may prove more interesting to give a brief sketch of one of the two other dramatic works of Kálidása that have come down to us.

Vikramorvasí describes the loves of the hero Purúravas and the celestial nymph Urvasí. The story is as old as the Rig Veda, and is in its first conception a myth of the Sun (Purúravas = bright-rayed) pursuing the Dawn (Urvasí = wide-expanding). But the origin of the story has long since been lost to the Hindus, and the Purúravas of Kálidása and the Puránas is a mortal king who rescued a celestial nymph named Urvasí from demons, and felt for her a tender love which was reciprocated. So smitten was the nymph with the charms of the mortal, that when she appeared in the court of Indra to enact a play, she forgot her part and betrayed her secret by uttering the name of the mortal she loved.

> "Urvasí played Lakshmí. Menaká was Varuní. The latter says—
>
> "Lakshmí, the mighty powers that rule the spheres
> Are all assembled; at their head appears
> The blooming Kesava; confess to whom
> Inclines your heart?
>
> "Her reply should have been—
>
> "'To Purushottama'; but instead of that—
> 'To Purúravas' escaped her lips."
>
> —WILSON'S TRANSLATION.

For this error the gentle nymph was punished; but Indra with considerate care modified the punishment into a blessing, and directed the nymph to go and live with her beloved mortal until he beheld an offspring borne by her.

Purúravas vainly tried to conceal his new love from his own queen, and expressed a penitence he did not feel by falling at her feet. The queen somewhat unceremoniously replied—

> "You make, my lord, an awkward penitent; I cannot trust you."
>
> —WILSON.

And she left the king to the very cruel but very wise reflection :—

> "I might have spared myself the pains. A woman is clear-sighted, and mere words touch not her heart. Passion must give them credit. The lapidary, master of his craft, with cold indifference eyes the spurious gem."—WILSON.

But the queen soon perceived that her husband's love was beyond control and her resentment was unavailing. With a Hindu wife's self-abnegation she contrived, under the guise of a religious performance, to make amends for her former behaviour. Clad in white, with only flowers for her ornaments, she came slowly to worship her lord and king, who almost felt a return of his previous fondness for her on seeing her in this attire.

"In truth she pleases me. Thus chastely robed in modest white, her clustering tresses decked with sacred flowers alone, her haughty mien exchanged for pure devotion; thus arrayed she moves with heightened charms."—WILSON.

But she knew her charms were unavailing; she presented oblations to the king, bowed, fell at his feet, rose, and then called the moon and the Rohiní star to

"Hear and attest the sacred promise that I make my husband. Whatever nymph attract my lord's regard, and share with him the mutual bond of love, I henceforth treat with kindness and complacency."—WILSON.

Even Urvasí's companion was struck with this magnanimous self-abnegation, and remarked—

"She is a lady of an exalted spirit, a wife of duty most exemplary."
—WILSON.

The loves of the king and the nymph and their temporary separation through a supernatural incident are then described with all the power of Kálidása's pen.

He pined during the separation, wandered in the forest, and addressed birds and beasts and inanimate objects—

"I have sued to the starry-plumed bird,
And the *koil* of love-breathing song;
To the lord of the elephant herd,
And the bee as he murmured along;

To the swan, and the loud waterfall,
  To the *chakwa*, the rock, and the roe;
In my search have I sued to them all,
  But none of them lightened my woe."—WILSON.

He recovered her after his wanderings, but was again likely to lose her. For the boy whom Urvasí had borne to her lord—but had concealed so long—was seen by chance by his father; and according to Indra's orders the nymph must return to the skies as soon as her lover saw the child she bore him. But Indra again modified his commands, and Nárada descended from the skies to carry Indra's mandate to Purúravas.

"And Urvasí shall be through life united
With thee in holy bonds."—WILSON.

Kálidása was a poet as well as a dramatist. Two of the best known Sanskrit epics are from his pen. One, the *Raghuvansa*, deals with the inexhaustible story of Ráma. In the other, the *Kumára Sambhava*, Kálidása paints from the storehouse of his own imagination the love of Umá for the great Siva, and their happy union. We have already alluded to this tale, but may return to it for the purpose of giving a few illustrative quotations.

Umá was born the daughter of the deity of the Himálaya mountains, and a sweeter child never saw the light—

"Blest was that hour, and all the world was gay,
When Mená's daughter saw the light of day.
A rosy glow filled all the brightening sky,
An odorous breeze came sweeping softly by,
Breathed round the hill a sweet unearthly strain,
And the glad heavens poured down their flowery rain."
—GRIFFITH'S TRANSLATION.

The early years of the gentle maiden are described with exquisite grace and sweetness; but a great future awaits her. The gods intend her as a bride to the mighty Siva, for unto them will be born a child who will lead the gods to victory against the Asuras. Siva is now engaged in pious contemplation in the Himálaya mountains, and it is arranged that the youthful Umá will wait on the mighty god as a handmaiden, and look to all his needs.

There is nothing lovelier and fresher in the creations of fancy than the image of Umá, clad in chaste garments and decorated with flowers, attending on the great god in his devotions, collecting flowers for him, and doing him due obeisance. In doing obeisance she stooped so low—

> "That from her hair,
> Dropped the bright flower that starred the midnight there."
> —GRIFFITH.

And Siva, pleased with her homage, blessed her—

> "Surely thou shalt be
> Blessed with a husband who loves none but thee."
> —GRIFFITH.

Everything might have gone on smoothly to the desired end, if the mischievous god of love had not interfered. He marks the moment of Siva's weakness and lets go his unerring shaft.

> "Like the moon's influence on the sea at rest,
> Came passion stealing o'er the hermit's breast,
> While on the maiden's lip that mocked the dye
> Of ripe red fruit he bent his melting eye,
> And oh! how showed the lady's love for him,
> The heaving bosom and each quivering limb!
> Like young Kadambas, when the leaf-buds swell
> At the warm touch of spring they love so well;
> But still with downcast eyes she sought the ground,
> And durst not turn their burning glances round.
> Then with strong effort Siva lulled to rest
> The storm of passion in his troubled breast,

And seeks, with angry eyes that round him roll,
Whence came the tempest o'er his tranquil soul.
He looked and saw the bold young archer stand,
His bow bent ready in his skilful hand,
Drawn towards the eye,—his shoulder well depressed,
And the left foot thrown forward as a rest.
Then was the hermit-god to madness lashed,
Then from his eye red flames of fury flashed.
So changed the beauty of that glorious brow,
Scarce could the gaze support its terror now.
Hark! heavenly voices sighing through the air:
'Be calm, great Siva, O be calm and spare!'
Alas! the angry eye's resistless flashes
Have scorched the gentle king of love to ashes!"

—GRIFFITH.

Love's bride laments the death of her lord, and Umá in mortification and grief retires into a wood to penance and prayer. The poet launches again into a description of the gentle and tender girl subjecting herself to hard penances unsuited to her frame. Summer is passed amid scorching fires—in autumn she remains exposed to the rains—and the blasts of winter see her still unshaken in her purpose.

A young hermit comes to inquire the reason of these severe penances undertaken by a young and tender damsel. Umá's maidens explain to him the cause, but the hermit can scarcely believe that so gentle a creature should be in love with so unlovable a god as Siva, who remains smeared with ashes and wanders about in funeral places—

"Impatient Umá listened; the quick blood
Rushed to her temples in an angry flood."

—GRIFFITH.

She explains to the unmannerly hermit with passionate eloquence the glories of the great deity whom none knows and none can comprehend, and she rises to depart from the place in anger and scorn—

> "She turned away, with wrath her bosom swelling
> Its vest of bark in angry pride repelling,—
> But sudden lo! before her wondering eyes,
> In altered form she sees the sage arise;
> 'Tis Siva's self before the astonished maid
> In all his gentlest majesty arrayed!"—GRIFFITH.

Yes, it is Siva himself, who had refused to be forced into love, but is now propitiated and pleased with Umá's penances, and humbly craves a return of his affection from the mountain maid.

Among the shorter poems of Kálidása, the best and sweetest is the *Meghadúta*, or the Cloud Messenger. The story is simple. A Yaksha is banished by royal order from his home for being too fond of his wife and neglecting his duties; and in his exile he gazes on the dark cloud of the rainy season and bids it carry a message of love to his dear beloved at home. The lover indicates the way by which the cloud should proceed, and the poet describes the various parts of India from the Vindhyas to the Himálaya mountains in verse, which, for richness of fancy and melody of rhythm, has never been excelled in the literature of the world:—

> "On Naga Nadi's banks thy waters shed,
> And raise the feeble jasmin's languid head.
> Grant for awhile thy interposing shroud,
> To where those damsels woo the friendly cloud;
> As while the garland's flowery stores they seek,
> The scorching sunbeams tinge their tender cheek,
> The ear hung lotus fades, and vain they chase,
> Fatigued and faint, the drops that dew the face.
> What though to northern climes thy journey lay,
> Consent to track a shortly devious way.

> To fair *Ujainí's* palaces and pride,
> And beauteous daughters turn awhile aside;
> Those glancing eyes, those lightning looks unseen,
> Dark are thy days, and thou in vain hast been."

Kálidása lived probably early in the sixth century, and some scholars identify him with the courtier Matrigupta, whom the great Vikramáditya helped to the throne of Kashmir. Another poet, Bháravi, lived later in the same century, and has left us one short epic, *Kirátárjuníyam*, a story of the penances by which Arjuna achieved the power to conquer his foes in the great war of the Kuru-Pándavas. Bháravi never equals Kálidása either in the power of a creative fancy or in true poetry and pathos, or even in melody or sweetness of verse; but he nevertheless possesses a vigour of thought and a spirited and lofty eloquence of expression which have made his works immortal.

The next century opens with the brilliant reign of Síláditya II., whom Houen Tsang found on the throne of Kanouj and of Northern India. Síláditya was himself an author, and has left us a drama, *Ratnávalí*, of much merity and beauty. A still more remarkable play, the *Nágánanda*, is also attributed to Síláditya II., but is, probably, like Ratnávalí, the work of some poet of his court. We call it a remarkable work, because it is probably the only Buddhist drama which has come down to us. In this Buddhist play we find Hindu gods and goddesses mixed up with Buddhist objects of veneration. It is this which gives the work its special value.

Jímútaváhana, prince of the Vidyádharas, finds Malayávatí, princess of the Siddhas, engaged in the worship of Gaurí (a Hindu goddess), and falls in love with her. He appears before her, as Dushyanta appeared before Sakuntalá, and is received with courtesy, and the maiden, we need hardly say, falls in love with the prince. The usual symptoms of love, as in Sakuntalá, affect Malayávatí; she is feverish, and sandal juice is applied to her person, and she is fanned with a plantain leaf.

Jímútaváhana employs himself with drawing a portrait of the maiden who had stolen his heart. He asks for a piece of red arsenic to draw the portrait, and his companion picks up from the ground and brings some pieces, from which five colours (blue, yellow, red, brown, and variegated) could be obtained. From this account it would appear that the ancient Hindus, like the ancient painters of Pompeii, used coloured earth and minerals for their painting.

Malayávatí watches the young prince as he draws the picture, and thinking it was the portrait of some other maiden whom he loved, becomes jealous and faints. In the meantime Malayávatí's father sends a message to Jímútaváhana offering his daughter as his bride, but Jímútaváhana does not yet know that the maiden he had seen was the princess herself, and desiring to be true to the maiden he had seen, refuses the hand of the princess.

The mistakes of both the lovers are soon removed. The prince discovers that the maiden with whom he had fallen in love is the very princess whose hand is offered to him; and the princess also soon discovers that the portrait which the prince had drawn is her own portrait. The wedding follows with great pomp and ceremony.

We have an amusing account here of a parasite of the king's court, Sekharaka, who had regaled himself too freely with wine during the festivities, and makes some ludicrous blunders. He declares that there are only two gods for him, Baladeva and Káma—the former being a Hindu god known for his drinking exploits, and the latter being the Hindu god of love; and the valiant knight goes out to meet his lady-love, a female slave with whom he is in love. Instead of meeting that damsel, he meets the prince's companion, a Bráhman, who had put his garment over his head to keep out insects, and so looked like a veiled woman. Sekharaka, not very keen in his perception, embraces the Bráhman as his mistress, to the utter disgust of the latter, who stops his nose at the smell of liquor! Confusion is worse confounded when the damsel herself appears on the spot; the not very discriminating lover is taxed with courting another maiden, and the Bráhman is treated to some choice epithets as "tawny monkey", has his sacred thread torn, and offers to fall at the feet of the slave girl in order to get out of the scrape. Everything, however, is at last explained satisfactorily.

We are then introduced to the bride and bridegroom in the raptures of their young love; the latter politely asks for a kiss in these words :—

> "O lovely one! If this face of thine with its pink flush as it is lighted up by the sun's rays, and with its soft down revealed by the spreading gleam of its teeth is really a lotus, why is not a bee seen drinking the honey from it?"—BOYD'S TRANSLATION.

But the lover is rudely interrupted by news about his kingdom, which takes him away.

So far the story is like the story of other Hindu plays. But the last two Acts are essentially Buddhistic, and illustrate, of course in an extravagant form, the real virtue of self-sacrifice for the good of others.

Jímútaváhana goes to the Western Gháts and sees on the seashore a heap of bones of Nágas, killed by Garuda, the king of birds. Nágas are snakes, but in the conception of Hindu and Buddhist poets they are formed like men, except that they are scaly and have hoods rising from their backs. A compact has been made with Garuda that a Nága will be sent to him daily for his food, and as Jímútaváhana sees a Nága tearing himself from his weeping mother and preparing himself as Garuda's food, his heart bleeds within him. He manages to offer himself up to the ferocious Garuda in place of the Nága, and the bird flies away with him.

There is wailing and lamentation in Jímútaváhana's household when the Nága runs there and reports that the prince has offered himself a sacrifice. His old parents and his newly-married wife rush to where Garuda was still eating the prince's flesh, his life all but extinct. The real Nága also rushes there and offers himself up to save the innocent prince.

Garuda then discovers his mistake and is horrified :—

"Alas! Alas! His own body has been of his own accord presented for my food by this noble-minded one, through pity to save the life of a Nága who had fallen within the reach of my voracity. What a terrible sin have I committed! In a word, this is a Bodhisatva whom I have slain."—BOYD'S TRANSLATION.

Jímútaváhana instructs Garuda how the sin can be expiated :—

"Cease for ever from destroying life ; repent of thy former deeds ; labour to gather together an unbroken chain of good actions by inspiring confidence in all living beings."—BOYD'S TRANSLATION.

The heroic prince expires after giving these instructions, as he had been more than half eaten up. His parents prepare to mount the funeral pyre to depart from this world. The lamenting young widow invokes Gaurí, the goddess, whom she had invoked before marriage.

All ends happily. Gaurí restores the prince to life; and Garuda prevails on Indra to revive to life all the Nágas whom he had killed before. *Harm not living creatures ;*—that is the moral of this Buddhist play.

Some eminent writers of fiction also flourished in this

reign. India was not better known to the ancient nations for her science and poetry than as the birthplace of fables and fiction. The oldest Aryan fables that are to be found anywhere are in the Buddhist *Játaka Tales*, dating from some centuries before Christ; and Dr. Rhys Davids has pointed out that many of them have travelled to Europe and have assumed various modern shapes.

Other fables, those of the *Panchatantra*, were probably current in India for many centuries before they were collected and compiled under that name. The compilation took place certainly before the sixth century, for in that century the compiled work was translated into Persian. The book was then translated into Arabic, Greek, and Hebrew; a Spanish translation appeared in the thirteenth and a German in the fifteenth century, and since then the work has been rendered into all the languages of Europe under the name of the Fables of Pilpay or Bidpai.

The fables of the Panchatantra are simple and entertaining, and are told in simple and easy Sanscrit prose. When we turn from them to the stilted and artificial style of the novelists of Síláditya's reign, we see at once the change which Sanscrit prose had undergone by the seventh century. Dandin wrote his *Dasakumára Charita*, or the Tales of the Ten Princes, probably early in that century, and his style is ornate and artificial. But it is in *Kádamvarí*, written by Bánabhatta, a courtier of Síláditya's court, that we find the beauties and faults of the style of the period in a marked degree. The story is wild and weird;—the same couple of lovers go through more than one life, and still feel the same irresistible attraction for each other; and scenes of overwhelming passion, intense sorrow, irresistible love, and austere penances in wild solitudes are depicted with power and a rare command of language. But the style, in spite of its wonderful power, is laboured and extravagant beyond all reasonable bounds, and often the same verbose sentence, with strings and adjectives and compound words, and with a profusion of figures of speech, runs through several pages. A shorter novel, *Vásavadattá*, was written by Subandhu in the same reign.

We have spoken of the drama and fiction of Síláditya's reign, but some poetical works composed in this period have also been handed down to us. Bhartrihari's *Satakas* are conspicuous among the productions of the Indian Muse for the terse and epigrammatic character of the poems. The *Satakas* show that Bhartrihari was a Hindu, but they are nevertheless marked by the Buddhist spirit of the time in which he lived. Professor Tawney has rendered some of them into elegant and spirited English verse, and a couple of extracts will convey an idea of the original to the reader :—

"Not to swerve from truth and mercy, not for life to stoop to shame;
From the poor no gifts accepting, nor from men of evil fame;
Lofty faith and proud submission,—who on fortune's giddy ledge
Firm can tread this path of duty, narrow as the sabre's edge?
Abstinence from sin of bloodshed, and from speech of others' wives,
Truth and open-handed largess, love for men of holy lives,
Freedom from desire and avarice,—such the path that leads to bliss,
Path which every sect may travel, and the simple cannot miss."

'Treachery is of crimes the blackest,
Avarice is a world of vice,
Truth is nobler far than penance,
Purity than sacrifice.

Charity's the first of virtues,
  Dignity doth most adorn,
Knowledge triumphs unassisted,
  Better death than public scorn.

You are a lord of acres
  But we are lords of song;
And we subdue the subtle,
  If you subdue the strong;
The rich of you are speaking,
  In me the wise believe,
And if you find me irksome,
  Why then—I take my leave.

What profit are the Vedas,
  Or books of legal lore,
Or those long-winded legends
  Repeated o'er and o'er?
What gain we by our merits?
  A dwelling in the skies—
A miserable mansion,
  That men of sense despise—
All these are huckstering methods—
  Give me that perfect way
Of self-contained fruition,
  Where pain is done away."

The same writer is also known as Bhatti, and is the author of *Bhattikávya*, which is the story of the Rámayana told so as to familiarize the reader with the most difficult conjugational forms of verbs. It is, in fact, a poetical work of considerable merit, composed to teach grammar!

A century passed by from the time of Síláditya, and then a great poet arose, a rival of Kálidása in merit and in fame. Bhavabhúti was born in Berar, but soon attached himself to the learned court of Kanouj, then the literary as well as the political capital of India. His *Málatímádhava* describes the love of a bold youth of his own native land, Berar, for a princess of Ujain, and the princess is won after many strange adventures powerfully described. His *Mahávirí Charita* is the story of the Rámayana from Ráma's boyhood to his wars in Ceylon, and return with Sítá to Oudh; and his *Uttara-Ráma Charita* continues the story of the epic to the exile and restoration of Sítá, and is the most powerful and pathetic composition in the Sanscrit language. The love and self-abnegation of gentle Sítá, the weakness of Ráma in sending her into exile, and the bitter contrition which follows, are described with a power which reminds the reader of the masterpieces of Shakespeare himself.

Of these plays, the first, the *Málatímádhava*, or the loves of Málatí and Mádhava, is the most original in plot.

Mádhava is the son of Devaráta, the minister of the poet's own country, Vidarbha or Berar, and has come to Padmávatí or Ujjayini to complete his studies. In that town, as he walked along the streets, Málatí, the daughter of the minister of the place,—

> "From her casement has beheld the youth,—he graceful as the god of love, herself love's blooming bride,—nor seen in vain."—WILSON'S TRANSLATION.

On the occasion of the annual festival of the god of love, the people flock to the shrine of love to pay their homage. Málatí, too, repairs to the shrine on an elephant, and meets Mádhava, and the youth and maiden gaze on each other, and fall in love.

But the course of true love never does run smooth; and the king of Padmávatí has promised Málatí's hand to a favourite, Nandana, and the king's minister, Málatí's father, dares not openly refuse his consent. The news is a terrible blow to the love-stricken maiden, and Kámandakí, a Buddhist priestess or abbess, exclaims in pity—

> "What can I aid? Fate and her sire alone exact obedience from a daughter. True, Sakuntalá, of Kusika's high race, bestowed

her love on a self-chosen lord—the king Dushyanta. A bright nymph of heaven espoused a mortal monarch Purúravas, and the fair princess, Vásavadattá, scorned the husband of her father's choice, and fled with prince Udayana. So poets tell, but these were desperate acts."—WILSON'S TRANSLATION.

It is quite apparent that the poet refers here to his great predecessor Kálidása's two works, and also to the story of Vásavadattá, which was so popular a theme of fiction and drama in the court of Síláditya II.

The Buddhist priestess, however, had made up her mind to help Málatí and Mádhava. They have an interview in the house of the priestess, but Málatí is torn away thence by the order of the queen. Mádhava in despair determines to have recourse to mysterious rites for gaining his end, and this leads us to a scene of awful Tántrika worship. The genius of Bhavabhúti never appears to greater advantage than when depicting a scene of magnificence or terror.

In a field in which dead bodies are burnt is situated a temple of the terrific goddess Chámundá, and the malignant priestess Kapála Kundalá, with her necklace of skulls (as her name implies), is engaged in worship. There goes Mádhava with his offering of raw flesh, to obtain from ghosts some help towards the attainment of his end. He offers the flesh to ghosts and goblins, and exclaims—

> "Now wake the terrors of the place, beset
> With crowding and malignant fiends; the flames
> From funeral pyres scarce lend their sullen light,
> Clogged with their fleshly prey, to dissipate
> The fearful gloom that hems them in. Pale ghosts
> Sport with foul goblins, and their dissonant mirths
> In shrill respondent shrieks is echoed round.
> Well, be it so. I seek and must address them.
> Demons of ill, and disembodied spirits,
> Who haunt this spot, I bring you flesh for sale;

The flesh of man, untouched by trenchant steel,
And worthy your acceptance. (*A great noise.*)
How the noise,
High, shrill and indistinct, of chattering sprites
Communicative, fills the charnel ground!
Strange forms like foxes flit along the sky:
From the red hair of their lank bodies darts
The meteor blaze; or from their mouths that stretch
From ear to ear, thickset with numerous fangs,
Or eyes or beards or brows, the radiance streams
And now I see the goblin host:

They mark my coming, and the half-chewed morsel
Falls to the howling wolf,—and now they fly.
(*Pauses, and looking round.*)
Race, dastardly as hideous! All is plunged
In utter gloom. The river flows before me,
The boundary of the funeral ground, that winds
Through mouldering bones its interrupted way.
Wild raves the torrent as it rushes past
And rends its crumbling banks; the wailing owl
Hoots through its skirting groves, and to the sounds
The loud long moaning jackal yells reply."—WILSON.

Suddenly Mádhava hears the voice, musical and wild, of a young woman in distress—

"Ah, cruel father! She you meant an offering
To the king's favour, now deserted dies."—WILSON.

That voice is not unfamiliar to Mádhava's ear; he bursts into the temple and finds Málatí dressed as a victím and about to be sacrificed by Aghoraghantá, the terrible priest of Chámundá. Some Tántrika rites require the sacrifice of a virgin—and the sweetest and purest virgin in Padmávati town had been selected and kidnapped for this sacrifice. Málatí herself does not know how she was stolen :—

"I reposed," she says,
"At eve upon the terrace: when I woke
I found myself a prisoner."—WILSON.

Mádhava rescues his beloved and slays the malignant priest. But the more malignant priestess Kapála Kundalá vows revenge.

We pass by a great many minor incidents. A friend of Mádhava, Makaranda by name, who is in love with Nandana's sister, disguises himself as Málatí, and is married to the king's favourite Nandana. The amorous husband comes to court his bride, but meets with rough usage which a maiden's arm could scarcely inflict! Nandana's sister then comes to teach her sister-in-law better manners, but finds her own beloved Makaranda as the pretended bride. An elopement follows; the king sends his guards to arrest the culprits; but Mádhava and his friend Makaranda beat back the guards, and the king generously forgives them in consideration of their valour.

Here the play might happily have ended with the marriage of the two pair of lovers with the king's sanction; but Bhavabhúti prolongs the story to bring in some powerful description of nature and of human feelings. His incidents and plot, as usual, are unnatural and extravagant, but his descriptions are matchless in power. Málatí is once more kidnapped by the foul priestess Kapála Kundalá, and Mádhava goes in search of her among the Vindhya mountains. Saudáminí, who was a Buddhist priestess before, but has now acquired supernatural powers by the practice of *Yoga*, resolves to help Mádhava; and from her lips we have a powerful description of the locality:—

"How wide the prospect spreads,—mountain and rock,
Towns, villages, and woods, and glittering streams!

There where the Párá and the Sindhu wind,
The towers and temples, pinnacles and gates,
And spires of Padmávatí, like a city
Precipitated from the skies, appear,
Inverted in the pure translucent wave.
There flows Lavaná's frolic stream, whose groves
By early rains refreshed, afford the youth
Of Padmavátí pleasant haunts, and where
Upon the herbage, bright'ning in the shower,
The heavy uddered kine contented browse.
Hark! how the banks of the broad Sindhu fall,
Crashing, in the undermining current,
Like the loud voice of thunder-laden clouds,
The sound extends, and like Heramba's roar,
As deepened by the hollow echoing caverns,
It floats reverberating round the hills.
Those mountains, coated with thick clustering woods
Of fragrant sandal and ripe Málúra
Recall to memory the lofty mountains
That southward stretch, where Godávari
Impetuous flashes through the dark deep shade
Of skirting forests, echoing to her fury."—WILSON.

Saudáminí by her magical powers rescues Málatí, and Málatí and Nandana's sister are happily wedded to Mádhava and Makaranda.

Bhavabhúti is the last of the galaxy of the poets of the Vikramádityan age, as Kálidása is the first. He lived in the court of King Yasovarman of Kanouj, but when that king was defeated in war by Lalitáditya, king of Kashmir, the poet accompanied the conqueror to Kashmir, and probably ended his days there about the middle of the eighth century.

The Dark Age then followed, and for three centuries India has no distinguished name in literature or in science. By the close of the eleventh century the modern Rajputs had become masters of India, and modern history begins with the Rajput revival.

INDEX.